UP CLOSE 2

English for Global Communication

Anna Uhl Chamot
Isobel Rainey de Diaz
Joan Baker-Gonzalez
with
Deborah Gordan & Nina Weinstein

THOMSON
HEINLE

Australia • Canada • Mexico • Singapore • Spain • United Kingdom • United States

Up Close, **Student Book 2**

Publisher, Global ELT: *Chris Wenger*
Acquisitions Editor: *Berta de Llano*
Developmental Editors: *Jean Pender, Ruth Ban*
Production Editor: *Sarah Cogliano*
Marketing Managers: *Amy Mabley, Ian Martin, Francisco Lozano*
Manufacturing Coordinator: *Mary Beth Hennebury*

Composition: *Graphic World*
Project Management: *Kris Swanson*
Illustration: *Ray Medici, Jane O'Conor*
Text Design: *Sue Gerould*
Cover Design: *Jim Roberts*
Printer: *C&C Offset Printing Co., Ltd.*

ISBN-13: 978-0-8384-3858-9
ISBN-10: 0-8384-3858-X

Photo Credits

Photos on the following pages are the exclusive property of Heinle:

Cover, 1, 4, 12, 14, 24, 32, 34, 42, 46, 56, 64, 66, 74, 76, 84, 85, 87, 88, 91, 93, 96, 98, 99, 106, 108, 116, 118, 119, 122, 132, 133, 134, 135, 136 (bottom)

Photos from other sources:

Page 3, upper left: © Michael S. Lewis/CORBIS

Page 3, lower middle: © Alexander C. Fields/CORBIS

Page 8, upper left: © Bettmann/CORBIS

Page 8, upper middle: © Bettmann/CORBIS

Page 8, upper right: © Bettmann/CORBIS

Page 8, lower left: © Hulton-Deutsch/CORBIS

Page 8, lower middle: © Bettmann/CORBIS

Page 8, lower right: © Bettmann/CORBIS

Page 13, upper left: © Dewitt Jones/CORBIS

Photos on the following pages are from PhotoDisc, Inc. Digital Imagery © copyright 2001 PhotoDisc, Inc.

3 (upper right), 38 (upper right, center right, lower left, lower right), 52, 55, 62, 107, 123, 136 (center)

Page 13, upper middle: © Bohemian Nomad Picturemakers/CORBIS

Page 13, upper right: © Robert Landau/CORBIS

Page 13, lower left: © Bill Ross/CORBIS

Page 13, lower right: © Ted Streshinsky/CORBIS

Page 38, upper left: RubberBall Productions 2000 ©

Page 38, center left: © CORBIS 2001

Page 136, top: © Philip James Corwin/CORBIS

Acknowledgments

The authors and publisher would like to acknowledge the contributions of the following individuals who reviewed the *Up Close* program at various stages of development and who offered helpful insights and suggestions:

Ana María Batis, Instituto de Educación de Aguascalientes, México

Rudy Bedon, Asociación Peruana de Profesores de Inglés, Perú

Marlene Brenes, Universidad Autónoma de Puebla, México

Jesús Cabrera, Instituto Cultural Dominico-Americano, República Dominicana

Nancy C. Carapaica, Centro Venezolano Americano, Venezuela

Chwun-Li Chen, Shih Chien University, Taipei, Taiwan

Freda Chiang, Yang Ming University, Taipei, Taiwan

Neil Cowie, Saitama University, Urawa, Japan

Sandra Davidson, Instituto Cultural Dominico-Americano, República Dominicana

Lúcia De Aragão, União Cultural Brasil-Estados Unidos, Brasil

Rocío Domínguez, Universidad Autónoma de Baja California, México

M. Sadiq Durrani, Centro Boliviano Americano, Bolivia

Guadalupe Espinoza, Universidad del Valle de México, México

Chiu-Hua Fiu, Van Nung College, Shingzuo, Taiwan

María Eugenia Flores, Centro Cultural Costarricense Norteamericano, Costa Rica

Fernando Fleurquin, Alianza Cultural Uruguay Estados Unidos, Uruguay

Clare Gilpin, Tokyo Junshin Women's College, Tokyo, Japan

Huiya Huang, National Ilan Institute of Technology, Ilan, Taiwan

Fatma Karaaslan, ANTYK ENG & BMT, Istanbul, Turkey

Kim A Ram, Seulgee Young-o-sa, Seoul, Korea

Kim Je Jung, English Campus, Seoul, Korea

Jiny Kim, Tiny Tots Institute, Seoul, Korea

Kim So Young, Mirae Young-o-sa, Seoul, Korea

Zoe Kinney, Instituto Cultural Dominico-Americano, República Dominicana

Lee Balk Eum, English Education Center, Seoul, Korea

Lee Bo Ram, English Education Center, Seoul, Korea

Ching-Ying Lee, Kang Ning Junior College, Taipei, Taiwan

Mary Meloy-Lara, Instituto John F. Kennedy, México

Michelle Merritt, Universidad de Guadalajara, México

Carroll Moreton, Ming Chuan University, Taipei, Taiwan

Dana Parkinson, Universidad de las Americas-Puebla, México

James Riordan, Associacão Cultural Brasil Estados Unidos, Brasil

Anthony Robins, Aichi University of Education, Kariya, Japan

Maritza Rodríguez, Asociación Peruana de Profesores de Inglés, Perú

Sergio Rodríguez, Instituto Tecnológico de Sonora, México

Elizabeth Ruiz, Universidad de Sonora, México

Consuelo Sanudo, Secretária de Educación Pública, México

Judith Shaw, Kansai Gaidai University, Oasaka, Japan

T. Nevin Siders, Universidad Nacional Autónoma de México, México

Kathryn Singh, Instituto Tecnologico y de Estudios Superiores de Monterrey, México

Eugenia Soto, Centro Cultural Costarricense Norteamericano, Costa Rica

Eric Ting, Kai Nan University, Tao Yuan, Taiwan

Pia María White, Universidad de Aguascalientes, México

CONTENTS

Cast of Characters

Casey Walker
Student at UCLA medical school

Stacey Walker
Model

Brad Garcia
Business Student at UCLA

Jason Garcia
Actor

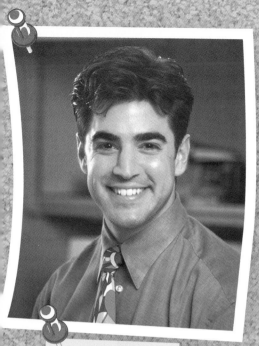

Mike Cohen
Webmaster

Ken Sato
Exchange Student from Japan

Andy Jordan

Susan Miller-Jordan
Teacher

Kevin Jordan
Doctor

Karen Sanders
Nurse

Nathan Sanders
Engineer

Phil Chen
Graphic Artist

Ben Wilson
Writer

Annie Davis
Apartment Manager

Practical Language

single
married
divorced
widowed

Talking about marital status and family

A: Are you married?
B: Yes, I am.
A: Do you have any children?
B: Yes, I have two. A boy and a girl.

A: Are you married?
B: No, I'm single.
A: Do you have any brothers or sisters?
B: No, I don't. I'm an only child.

Personal identification

This is Meg Young.

This is her student identification (or student ID).

Her **full name** is Margaret Ann Young-Stewart.

Her **last name** or **maiden name** is Young.

She hyphenates her **married name** Young-Stewart.

Her **first name** is Margaret, but her **nickname** is Meg.

Her **middle name** is Ann.

Her **middle initial** is A.

Classroom instructions

1. Sit with a partner.
2. Form a group of three.
3. Stand up and move to your group.
4. Sit down, please.
5. Come to the board, please.
6. Point to the book.
7. Read this sentence aloud.
8. Write these words.

Please print all information.

Class: _Contemporary Dance 101_

Teacher _Mr. Ascher_

Name _Young-Stewart_   _Margaret_   _A._
         (last)   (first)   (middle initial)

Address: _2105 E. Park Road_
                    (street)

Winfield,   _New York_   _11500_
   (city)   (state)   (zip)

Telephone: _659-1245_   Sex: M (F)

Identifying people's physical appearance...

A: I'd like to meet that man.
B: Which one?
A: The short one.

A: Where's Ken?
B: Over there next to the tall man.
A: Which one?
B: The one with the glasses.

by height

He's the short one.

He's the tall one.

by use of glasses

the man with
the glasses

the one
without glasses

by hair color and length

the boy with
long, blond hair

the boy with
short, black hair

the boy with
short, red hair

by clothing

the tall girl
in the pink dress

the tall girl
in the blue skirt

Great movie!

Communication Goals	Grammar Goals	Vocabulary Goals
Talking about past events	Regular and irregular simple past	Movie types
Making invitations		Descriptive adjectives
Talking about movies	*Yes/No* and *wh-* questions with short answers	*Did you have a good time?*
		It was okay.
		It was scary.

1 Warm Up

A. PAIR WORK Look at the pictures. How often do you go to the movies? How often do you go to concerts? How often do you eat out? Ask a partner.

B. Listen. Where did the people go? Check the correct picture.

1. _____

2. _____

3. _____

C. GROUP WORK Make a list. Where do people go on dates? Think of ten places. Order your list (1 = the most fun place; 10 = the least fun place).

2 Conversation

Getting to know you

Jason and Casey are on their first date. First, they saw a movie. Now they're at a restaurant.

A. Listen and practice.

1.

So, did you like the movie?

Yes, I did. I liked it a lot. Did you enjoy it?

It was alright. I closed my eyes. I don't like horror movies very much.

2.

I didn't know that. I'm sorry about the movie.

Oh, that's okay. It wasn't so bad.

Well, here are our drinks.

3.

Oh, no! What did I do? I spilled my drink all over you! I'm so sorry!

It's okay. Don't worry about it.

4.

Look, why don't we go for a walk?

I'm sorry. I can't. It's late, and I have a test tomorrow. I studied last night, but I didn't study a lot.

I blew it!
= I made a mistake!

5.

That was a great date!

Oh, no. I blew it!

B. Discuss. Did Jason enjoy his date with Casey? Did Casey enjoy her date with Jason? Explain your answers.

3 Grammar in Context

Talking about past events

Past tense verbs	
Simple past of regular verbs	**Simple past of irregular verbs**

Simple past of **regular** verbs:

spill → spill**ed**
start → start**ed**
look → look**ed**

BUT

like → lik**ed**
study → stud**ied**

Simple past of **irregular** verbs:

drive → **drove**
go → **went**
see → **saw**
have → **had**

BUT

be → I/he/she/it **was**
be → you/we/they **were**

Practice

A. PAIR WORK Complete the sentences. Use the past tense of the verbs in the box.

close	walk	study	hand	spill	look

1. Jason _____ a drink on Casey.　**4.** They _____ at each other.

2. He _____ Casey a napkin.　**5.** Casey _____ her eyes during the movie.

3. They _____ home.　**6.** They _____ the menu at the restaurant.

B. Match the sentences with the pictures below. Write the numbers.

a. _____

b. _____

c. _____

d. _____

e. _____

f. _____

Pronunciation

C. **Listen and check the ending you hear.**

Past tense endings		
/t/	→	liked
/d/	→	spilled
/id/	→	wanted

	/t/	/d/	/id/
1. handed			
2. spilled			
3. watched			
4. looked			
5. closed			
6. wanted			
7. listened			
8. studied			

D. **Listen again and repeat.**

1. Jason handed Casey her drink.
2. Jason spilled the drink on Casey.
3. They looked at each other.
4. He really liked her.
5. Casey closed her eyes.
6. Casey wanted to go home.
7. Jason listened to her.
8. Casey studied a lot.

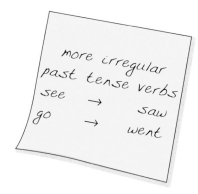

more irregular
past tense verbs
see → saw
go → went

 Interact

E. **Write some sentences about your weekend. Use the suggestions below to help you.**

Example: *I saw a movie with my friends.*

1. went to a restaurant
2. played tennis
3. studied for a test
4. watched TV
5. went to a party

_____

_____

_____

_____

_____

_____

_____

F. PAIR WORK **Talk about your weekend.**

4 Grammar in Context

Asking and telling about past events

Simple past tense						

Yes/No questions

Did	I you he/she/it we you they	eat dinner at 5:00?

Short answers

Yes,	I you he/she/it	did.
No,	we you they	didn't.

Wh- questions

What		I you he	do last night?
When	did	she it	start?
Where		we they	go?

Responses

I You He	went to a movie.
She It	started at 9:00 p.m.
We They	went to L.A.

Practice

A. Complete the sentences about Jason and Casey.

Example: Jason and Casey __*went*__ on a date. They __*didn't stay*__ home.
(go)   (not / stay)

1. They _____ a horror movie. They _____ TV.
(see)   (not / watch)

2. Casey _____ the movie. Jason _____ it a lot.
(not / enjoy)   (like)

3. Jason and Casey _____ drinks. They _____ their drinks.
(order)   (not / have)

4. Jason _____ the date to end. Casey _____ to go home.
(not / want)   (need)

Interact

B. GROUP WORK Ask and answer questions about what you did last night.

What did you do on Saturday night?

Did you have a good time?

Talking about movies

Comedies are **funny**.

Action movies are **fast-moving** and **exciting**.

Horror movies are **scary**.

Westerns are about the American West in the 19th century. They're **exciting**, too.

Dramas are stories about people's problems. Sometimes they're **romantic**. Sometimes they're **sad**.

Science fiction movies are often about the future. They are **interesting**.

Stacey:	What kind of movie did you see?
Casey:	We saw a horror movie.
Stacey:	Was it scary?
Casey:	Yes. It was really scary.

More irregular
past tense verbs
write → wrote
read → read
meet → met

 ## Listening

A. Listen. What kind of movie did each person see? Number the movies you hear.

_____ drama
_____ horror
_____ Western
_____ action
_____ science fiction
_____ comedy

CULTURE UP CLOSE

Movie ratings in the U.S.

G	General Audiences: Anyone can see this movie.
PG-13	Parental Guidance: Suggested for children under 13.
R	Restricted: People under 17 may only go with a parent or guardian.
NC-17	Only people over 17 may see this movie.

Practice

B. PAIR WORK Choose two types of movies from page 8.
Give two examples of each movie type.

Example: science fiction
        1. *Star Wars*
        2. *ET*

Interact

C. PAIR WORK Take turns inviting each other to a movie.
Use the movies from Exercise B above.

Examples:

A: Why don't we see *Star Wars* tonight?	**A:** Why don't we see a movie tonight?
B: I'm sorry. I can't	**B:** Great. What do you want to see?
A: Well, how about Friday night?	**A:** How about a science fiction movie?
B: Friday? I'd love to. OR Friday? I'm sorry. I'm busy.	**B:** I'd love to. How about *Star Wars*?
	A: Great!

LANGUAGE UP CLOSE

Invitations	Yes	No
Why don't we + *verb*? How about + *noun*?	(Great.) I'd love to.	(I'm) Sorry. I can't.

6 Listening in Context

A. Listen. Circle the types of movies showing at the Golden Theater.

a. comedy   b. horror   c. science fiction   d. Western

B. Write the show times for each movie.

Love Letters   _____   _____
Monsters Never Sleep   _____   _____
Indian Territories   _____   _____

C. Read the information below. Listen again. Which movie do you think each person saw? Check the theater.

	Theater 1	Theater 2	Theater 3
1. Casey saw a funny movie.	_____	_____	
2. Jason saw a cowboy movie.	_____	_____	_____
3. Andy saw a scary movie.	_____	_____	_____

7 Reading

A magazine article

Before you read

A. PAIR WORK Look at the list of dating problems. Check (√) the most common problems. Name other problems. Compare your answers with a partner.

Your date:

1. _____ was late.

2. _____ didn't have a sense of humor.

3. _____ didn't offer to pay for dinner.

4. _____ wasn't interesting.

5. _____ came the wrong day.

6. _____ canceled at the last minute.

not interesting = boring

While you read

B. Read the magazine article. Circle the best title.

1. The Perfect Date   **2.** Oh, no!   **3.** A Happy Ending

Laura Nelson was twenty-two years old. She was originally from Detroit, Michigan, but she lived in Los Angeles.

Laura worked for a computer company, Glendale Computers. She met Tyler Sofer at work. Tyler was tall and good looking, and Laura really liked him.

One day, Tyler asked Laura out on a date. Of course, she said, "I'd love to."

Their date was at 8:00 p.m. Tyler was an hour late.

They went to a Western movie, but Laura didn't like the movie at all.

They decided to have dinner at an Italian restaurant. When the waitress brought their food, there was a dead fly on Laura's spaghetti. Tyler tried to pay for the dinner, but he didn't have enough money. So, Laura had to pay.

After dinner, Tyler drove Laura to the beach. It started to rain. They went back to the car, but it had a flat tire. Tyler changed the tire and drove Laura home.

"I'm really sorry," Tyler said. "Why don't we try this again? How about next Friday?"

"Sure," Laura said. The next date had to be better, she thought.

The next date was fine. Then the date after that was even better. Two years later, they got married. Laura and Tyler celebrated their 5th wedding anniversary last Sunday.

After you read

C. PAIR WORK Work with a partner. Write the problems Laura had on the date. Rate the problems from 1 to 6. (1 = not a very bad problem; 6 = a very bad problem)

Problem	Rating
Tyler was late.	3

D. GROUP WORK Discuss these questions about dating behavior.

1. In this story, Tyler asked Laura out on a date. In the United States, men can ask women out. Women can also ask men out. In your country, do women ask men out on dates?
2. Tyler tried to pay for dinner. He didn't have enough money. In the United States, men or women can pay when they go on a date. In your country, who usually pays?

8 Writing

A narrative

Before you write

A. GROUP WORK Look at these pictures. Discuss the questions below.

1. Is this the beginning or end of each date? Explain your answer.
2. Do these people like each other? Explain your answer.
3. Describe how the people look. Are they happy? Are they having a good time? Explain.

Write

B. The pictures above are all from first dates. Write about what you think happened.

> Example: They went to a science fiction movie. He didn't like the movie. They decided to go to a café . . .

Putting It Together

A. Write the title of the last movie you saw. What kind of movie was it? When did you see it? What did you think of it?

_____

_____

_____

B. GROUP WORK Ask three classmates about the last movie they saw. Fill in the chart. Tell them about your movie.

Name	Movie title	When they saw it	What they thought

Where's the Walk of Fame?

Communication Goals	Grammar Goals	Vocabulary Goals
Describing location	Prepositions of location	Directions
Asking about location	*There is/are + one/a lot of/any*	*I'm really sorry.*
Asking for and giving directions		*I'm so glad.*
		How do I get to . . .?

1 Warm Up

A. GROUP WORK Look at the pictures. Read the names out loud. How much do you know about these places? Discuss with your classmates.

1. _____

Mann's Chinese Theater

2. _____

Beverly Hills Hotel

3. _____

Getty Museum

4. _____

Walk of Fame

5. _____

Hollywood Bowl

 B. Jason wants to go sightseeing. What does he want to see? Listen and check the pictures above.

2 Conversation

Where's the Walk of Fame?

Jason and Brad are looking for the Walk of Fame. Stacey and Casey are looking for the Walk of Fame, too.

A. Listen and practice.

1.
- How was your date with Casey last night?
- It was awful. I blew it.
- I'm really sorry, Jason.
- Thanks . . . Hey, where are we? Let's ask for directions.

1.
- How was your date with Jason last night?
- It was great.
- I'm so glad.
- Thanks . . . I think we're lost. Why don't we ask for directions?

2.
- Excuse me. Where's the Walk of Fame?
- It's on Hollywood Boulevard, between Vine Street and Fairfax Avenue.

2.
- Excuse me. Can you tell us how to get to the Walk of Fame?
- Sure. Go south on Highland Ave., and turn right at the first corner. That's Hollywood Blvd.
- Thanks.

3.
- Go north on Highland Avenue, and turn left on Hollywood Blvd. The Walk of Fame is right there.
- Thank you.

4.
- Casey, what are you doing here?
- Jason! Hi! It's great to see you!

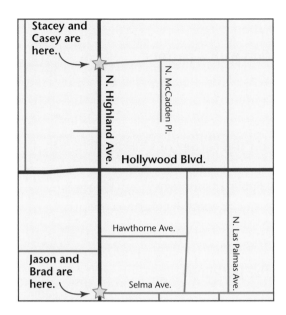

B. Look at the map. Read the conversation again.

1. Find Jason and Brad's position on the map and trace their way to the Walk of Fame.
2. Find Casey and Stacey's position on the map and trace their way to the Walk of Fame.

3 Grammar in Context

Describing location

Prepositional phrases

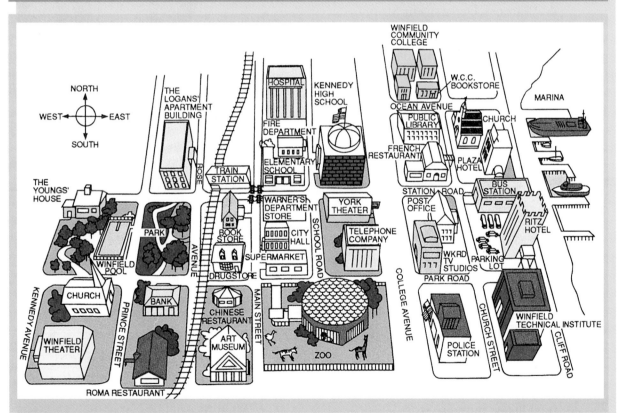

The bus station is **next to** the Ritz Hotel.

The bus station is **between** the Plaza Hotel and the Ritz Hotel.

The Plaza Hotel is **on the corner.**

The bus station is **near** the Marina.

 Practice

A. **PAIR WORK** Listen and practice the conversation with a partner.

> **Jason:** Where's Community College?
> **Brad:** It's **at the end of** College Avenue. It's **on the corner of** College and Ocean.
> **Jason:** Where's the college bookstore?
> **Brad:** It's **on** Church Street, **across from** the Public Library. Why?
> **Jason:** Casey's a medical student. I want to get a book about medicine for her.

B. **PAIR WORK** Ask and answer questions about the buildings and places on the map on page 15.

1. the police station / College Avenue
2. Kennedy High School / Station Road and College Avenue
3. the fire department / School Road / the elementary school and the hospital
4. Warner's Department Store / Main Street and Station Road
5. the Chinese restaurant / Park Road / Rose Avenue and Main Street

C. Look at the map on page 15. Fill in the blanks with words from the box.

to the right / left of	next to	near	across from
at the end of	on the corner of	on	between

1. The telephone company is _____ Park Road and College Avenue.
2. The bus station is _____ the Ritz Hotel.
3. Community College is _____ College Avenue.
4. City Hall is _____ the supermarket and Warner's Department Store.
5. The post office is _____ the Plaza Hotel.
6. The art museum is _____ Main Street.
7. WKRD TV Studios is _____ the telephone company.
8. The telephone company is _____ the York Theater.

Listening

D. Listen for the location of each store. Add the store names to the map.

| electronics store | shoe store | toy store | gift shop | jewelry store |

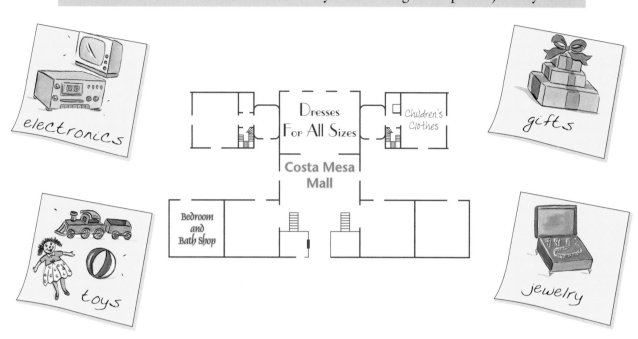

electronics

Dresses For All Sizes

Children's Clothes

Costa Mesa Mall

Bedroom and Bath Shop

toys

gifts

jewelry

 Pronunciation

E. Listen to the stressed words.

It's **on** the **left**. It's **near** the **store**.

F. Listen again. Underline the stressed words. Then repeat.

1. It's on Fifth Avenue.
2. It's across from the bank.
3. They're on Center Street.
4. It's between the bank and the post office.
5. It's on the right.
6. It's next to a hotel.

4 Grammar in Context

Asking about location

There is/are + a/one/a lot of/any

Ken: **Are there any** restaurants in Santa Maria?
Phil: Yes, **there are. There are a lot of** restaurants.
Ken: Where are they?
Phil: **There's a** nice Italian restaurant on Main Street.
Ken: **Is there a** Japanese restaurant, too?
Phil: Yes, **there is. There's one** on Santa Monica Avenue.

Practice

A. PAIR WORK Use the map on page 15. Take turns asking for and giving information about the places below.

Example: a hospital
- **A:** *Are there any hospitals in Santa Maria?*
- **B:** *Yes, there are.*
- **A:** *Where are they?*
- **B:** *There's one on Main Street.*

1. police station
2. fire department
3. train station
4. parks

5. schools
6. colleges
7. supermarket
8. hotels

LANGUAGE UP CLOSE

Contractions
There's = there is
There isn't = there is not

Interact

B. PAIR WORK Think of five places in your town; for example: restaurants, museums, clothing stores. Take turns being a tourist. Ask for information about the places.

Is there a zoo in _____?

No, there isn't.

Are there any hotels in _____?

Yes, there are. There's one on _____.

5 Vocabulary in Context

Asking for and giving directions

A. Listen to the conversation.

It's Saturday. Ken is on Melrose Avenue. He wants to go to Capitol Records. He asks a police officer for directions.

Ken:	Excuse me. **How do I get to** Capitol Records from here?
Officer:	Excuse me?
Ken:	**Can you tell me how to get to** Capitol Records?
Officer:	**Go east on** Melrose. **Go to** Vine Street. **Turn left on** Vine. Capitol Records is **right there**.
Ken:	Thanks, officer.

B. PAIR WORK Use the map
to ask for and give directions.

1. to the Walk of Fame from
   the Jim Henson Company
2. to the Hollywood Bowl from
   Capitol Records
3. to Mann's Chinese Theater
   from the Hollywood Bowl
4. to the All-Star Café from
   Mann's Chinese Theater
5. to the Hollywood Athletic
   Club from the Walk of Fame
6. to the Walk of Fame from
   the Hollywood Athletic Club

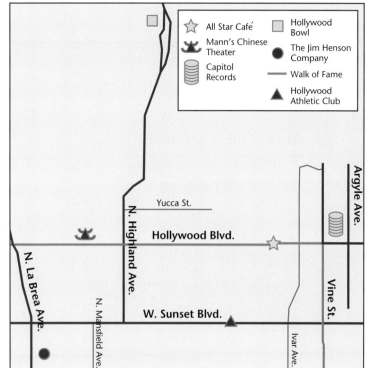

 Interact

C. PAIR WORK Make a map from your school to a place nearby.
Give your partner the directions. Have your partner make a map.
Compare maps. Did your partner draw it correctly?

6 Listening in Context

A. Listen. What does Jason want to do? Circle the correct answer.

   a. meet the stars   **b.** have a salad   **c.** go to a movie

B. Listen again. Write the directions to Salads of the Stars.

7 Reading

A subway map

Before you read

A. Answer these questions.

1. Is there a subway system in your city or country?
2. Why do people use subways?
3. Why do some people prefer the bus?

The most common things people forget on a subway are: umbrellas, house keys, books, jackets or coats, cellular phones, purses, and wallets.

commuter train = train for people going to work

ctr. = center

main = most important

change = go from one to another

While you read

B. Study the map of the subway system in Boston, Massachusetts to find:

1. the two kinds of lines on the map.
2. the four subway lines.
3. the four main stations where people can change subway lines.

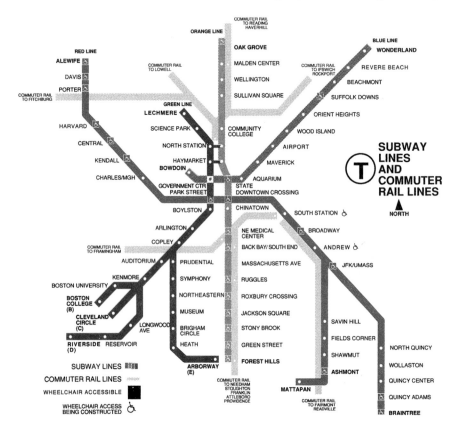

After you read

C. PAIR WORK Use the map of the Boston subway system to give directions.

Example: *From Broadway to State*

Go north on the Red Line. Change at Downtown Crossing. Take the Orange Line and go north. State is the first stop.

1. from Boston University to Harvard
2. from Airport to Central
3. from Harvard to Arlington
4. from North Station to Revere Beach
5. from Mattapan to Chinatown

Writing

Directions

Before you write

A. GROUP WORK Ask your classmates: Where do you live?

Write

B. Write detailed directions from school to the house of someone in your group. Add their address at the end of your directions.

Address:

9 Putting It Together

A. PAIR WORK Look at the map of the zoo below. You are at the Lakeside Café. Ask each other for directions to get to five places.

Map labels:

North Way

Government Drive

N
W   E
S

Bears

Spring Drive

Children's Zoo

North Parking Lot

The Living World Entrance

Lakeside Café

Rest room

Monkeys and Gorillas

Elephants

Circle Drive

Reptiles

Rest room

West Drive

South Drive

East Drive

Birds

River Drive

River's Edge Exhibit

Insects

Rest room

Seals

South Gate

River Drive

B. GROUP WORK Now take turns giving directions between two places in your city or town.

Stay TUNED

What are they going to do?

We're jogging at Griffith Park.

Communication Goals	Grammar Goals	Vocabulary Goals
Talking about healthy eating habits and exercise	Simple present vs. present continuous	Exercise verbs
Making suggestions	Negative questions	*I am in great shape.*
Making excuses	Statements with *because*	*Really?*
Giving explanations		*Why don't we . . .?*

1 Warm Up

©ULTURE UP CLOSE

A. Look at the chart. Can you do the exercises for your age?

How healthy are you?	
Age 16–19	fifty sit-ups, twenty-five push-ups
Age 20–29	forty sit-ups, twenty push-ups
Age 30–39	thirty sit-ups, fifteen push-ups
Age 40–49	twenty-five sit-ups, ten push-ups
Age 50–59	twenty sit-ups, seven push-ups

54% of Americans exercise regularly. Their favorite forms of exercise are walking, swimming, and playing tennis.

sit-ups

push-ups

I can try. . . .

Eating . . . can improve your health.

. . . is good.

B. PAIR WORK Talk with a partner about three ways to improve your health.

2 Conversation

I love to exercise. Really.

A. Listen and practice.

Annie and Ben are at Griffith Park. They're jogging.

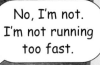

1.

Do you go jogging often?

This is an easy hill.

Easy? It's a mountain!

Well, yes. Yes, I do. I jog every day.

2. Ben, slow down. You're running too fast.

No, I'm not. I'm not running too fast.

3.

I'm in great shape. I go to the gym three times a week.

I'm worried about you, Ben. Let's take a break.

I don't need a break. I'm doing fine.

Really?

4. I'm slowing down because I'm wearing new shoes. That's the problem.

Yeah, right.

B. Answer the questions.

1. What are Annie and Ben trying to do?
2. Is it easy or difficult . . .
   a. for Annie?
   b. for Ben?

How do you know?

3 Grammar in Context

Talking about healthy eating habits and exercise

Simple present vs. present continuous

Ben **eats** a lot.

Ben **is eating** lunch now.

Annie **jogs** three times a week, and she**'s jogging** now.

Practice

A. PAIR WORK Take turns. Talk about your healthy
and unhealthy habits.

Example: lose weight

1. exercise more
2. eat less
3. eat more vegetables
4. eat more fruit
5. get more sleep

Do you want
to lose weight?

Yes, I do.

Are you trying to
lose weight now?

No, I'm not.

Listening

B. Listen to these different recorded telephone messages.
Fill out the chart below with the information you hear.

Who's doing what?						
Annie	**Jason**	**Casey**	**Stacey**	**Brad**	**Ben**	**Ken**

C. PAIR WORK Take turns asking and answering questions
about the people on the chart.

Example: *Where's Annie?*   *What does Brad do everyday?*

She's jogging at the park.   *He* _____.

Interact

D. PAIR WORK Write a short message for your telephone
answering machine. Explain that you are out. You can also
say what you are doing. Ask callers to leave you a message.
Then, read your message to your partner. Take turns.

E. PAIR WORK Switch partners with another pair of students.
Tell your new partner what your first partner is doing.

4 Grammar in Context

Making suggestions and excuses

Why don't . . . ?	
Annie:	Why don't you exercise more?
Ben:	Because I'm in great shape. I don't need to.
Jason:	Why don't we go swimming?
Brad:	I can't. I have to study.
Ken:	Why don't we go jogging?
Mike:	Sure. Let's go.

Practice

A. Match the suggestions and questions to the appropriate responses.

1. Why don't we go for a walk?
2. Why don't you eat more vegetables?
3. Why don't we have fish for lunch?
4. Why don't we play basketball?
5. Why don't you ever go swimming?

_____ Because I can't swim.

_____ Well, I had it yesterday. Let's have something else.

_____ Because I don't like vegetables.

_____ It's starting to rain. Let's go later.

_____ We can't. We don't have a ball.

Interact

B. PAIR WORK Take turns. Make suggestions like the ones above, using the information below. Your partner can give a different response for each suggestion. Take turns.

eat out tonight / go away for the weekend / play golf this afternoon / go shopping this Saturday / go to the movies tonight

5 Vocabulary in Context

reps = repetitions

Exercising

jog /
go for a run

swim laps

lift weights

do (ten) reps

work out

be in great shape

Practice

A. **Use some of the expressions from page 27 to complete the following conversations. Your answers will vary.**

Annie: Let's go _____.

  Ben: Sure, I love to exercise.

Annie: Do you _____ much?

  Ben: Yes, I do. My routine includes _____ of push-ups and sit-ups.

Annie: Do you _____?

  Ben: Yeah. And I try to _____ at least once a week.

B. **PAIR WORK** **Practice your conversations.**

 ## Pronunciation

C. **Listen. You will hear each sentence twice, first in slow speech and then in natural speech.**

1. Why don't we try to get more exercise?
2. Don't you go to the gym every day?
3. You need to exercise more.
4. I want to go for a run.
5. Do you want to go jogging?
6. Do you like to swim?
7. Why don't we go to the park?
8. She needs to get more sleep.

D. **Listen again. Notice the different pronunciations of *to*.**

E. **Listen again and repeat.**

> **LANGUAGE UP CLOSE**
>
> *To* is pronounced /t+ə/ in natural (fast) speech when it is followed by a word.

CULTURE UP CLOSE

In the U.S., there are 29.5 million health-club members. In Europe, there are 16.4 million, and in the rest of the world, 5 million.

 Interact

F. GROUP WORK Find two classmates who do the following activities. Write their names in the correct box. Write down how often they do the activity.

Do you jog sometimes?

Not every day, but I jog often.

Find someone who . . .		
jogs everyday	plays soccer once a week	works out
likes to play tennis	swims regularly	eats healthy meals
walks to school or work	lifts weights	plays basketball

 **6 Listening in Context**

A. Read the questions below. Listen to the news report for the correct answers.

1. American eating habits are changing.   Yes   No

2. How many Americans used to be considered overweight?

3. How many Americans are considered overweight today?

4. Who did the report on physical activity?

5. What percentage (%) of Americans don't exercise regularly?

6. What percentage (%) of Americans don't exercise at all?

B. PAIR WORK Compare your answers with a partner.

C. GROUP WORK Discuss the following questions. Are Americans in good shape? How do they compare to most people you know?

7 Reading

Eating and exercise habits

LANGUAGE UP CLOSE

Obese is a word usually used by doctors. It means very, very heavy.

Before you read

A. Look at the title of this article. What is the article about?

B. What do you think? Is it better to be heavy and exercise regularly, or thin and not exercise? Why?

While you read

C. Find out which is better for your health: to be heavy and exercise regularly, or to be thin and not exercise.

Heavy and Exercising Regularly, or Thin and Not Exercising— Which is better for your health?

Samantha Rogers, a New York writer in her late 30s, is a big woman. She tries to eat healthy food. She sleeps well, and she goes jogging almost every day. She's 5 feet 11 inches (180 centimeters) tall and 205 pounds (93 kilos). However, according to the United States government, Rogers is obese.

The question for Rogers and others is this: Can a person be both in great shape and heavy?

Doctors can't agree on the definition of good health.

Doctors and health professionals discussed that question at a meeting of the American College of Sports Medicine this month.

Dr. Roberta Sinclair, an obesity researcher at the University of Quebec, feels that exercise alone cannot stop heart disease. "Samantha Rogers is exercising. This is good. But she also needs a low-fat diet to help her lose 25 to 30 pounds (11 to 13 kilos)," said Dr. Sinclair. "With obesity there is a major risk of heart trouble."

Dr. Steven N. Johnson, a doctor with the Dallas Medical Institute, disagrees. "Her exercise routine is improving her health," Dr. Johnson said. "She's better heavy and exercising, than thin and not exercising." Dr. Johnson studied 25,000 people who were overweight and of average weight. He found that exercise is better for your health than no exercise. Dr. Johnson pointed to his own body. "Some people can't lose weight," he said. "I run everyday, but I'm still heavy."

To conclude, it seems as if even doctors can't agree on the definition of good health.

After you read

D. Read the following questions. Skim the story again to find the answers.

1. Which doctor believes it's OK to be heavy and exercise regularly?
2. Which doctor thinks it's better to lose more weight?

E. Circle the correct answer.

1. Samantha Rogers is a . . .
   a. teacher.   b. writer.   c. researcher.

2. She's . . .
   a. 5′ 6″ and 139 pounds.   b. 5′ 2″ and 227 pounds.   c. 5′ 11″ and 205 pounds.

3. She jogs . . .
   a. every day.   b. almost every day.   c. never.

4. Doctors met at the . . .
   a. University   b. University   c. American College
      of Chicago.   of Quebec.   of Sports Medicine.

5. Dr. Sinclair wants Samantha Rogers to lose . . .
   a. 25-30 pounds.   b. 5-10 pounds.   c. nothing.

6. Dr. Johnson thinks Samantha Rogers should . . .
   a. lose more weight.   b. exercise more often.   c. keep the same lifestyle.

8 Writing

Supporting an opinion

A. GROUP WORK Choose one of the opinions below. Think of three reasons to support your choice.

1. It's better to be heavy and exercising regularly.
2. It's better to be thin and not exercising.

Write

B. List your group's three reasons. Compare your group's opinion and reasons with other groups.

9 Putting It Together

A. PAIR WORK Answer the following questions. Then turn your book to check your answers. Compare your answers.

QUESTIONNAIRE

Am I a healthy eater?

1. How often do you eat vegetables?

   a. every day   **b.** three times a week   **c.** every week

2. How often do you have drinks with caffeine?

   a. once or twice a month   **b.** once or twice a week   **c.** every day

3. How often do you eat junk food?

   a. once every few months   **b.** once or twice a month   **c.** more than once a week

4. How often do you eat cake for dessert?

   a. always   **b.** sometimes   **c.** seldom

5. How often do you eat red meat?

   a. never or hardly ever   **b.** more than once a week   **c.** almost every day

Every *a* answer = 3 points.
Every *b* answer = 2 points.
Every *c* answer = 1 point.

Am I a healthy eater?

points	eating habits!
11–15 points	You are a healthy person. Well done! Stay healthy!
8–11 points	You are an average eater.
Less than 8	Your diet is unhealthy. You should change your

caffeine drinks

junk food

dessert

red meat

Stay TUNED

Why does Stacey look unhappy?

B. PAIR WORK Add your points. Turn your book around to read the information in the box. Compare your answers with a partner.

They want a taller model.

Communication Goals	Grammar Goals	Vocabulary Goals
Asking for and getting information in a store Making comparisons Explaining problems with clothes Making choices	Adjectives of comparison *too* + adjective *a/an/the* + adjective + *one*	Clothes *They're on sale.* *That's crazy.* *What's the problem?*

1 Warm Up

A. Label the pictures using the clothing vocabulary below.

tie	jacket	shirt	pants	shoes	sweater
skirt	boots	coat	hat	gloves	hood

B. PAIR WORK Work with a partner. Make a list of the clothes your partner is wearing.

C. Listen. Circle the names of the clothes you hear.

tie	skirt	cap	boots
jacket	sweater	dress	hat
top	pants	jeans	hood

D. GROUP WORK Discuss. What clothes do you like to wear?

2 Conversation

Can I try a shorter length?

A. Listen and practice.

Stacey and Casey are trying on clothes at a store.

1. So, how do those pants fit?

Um, I think they're too long. Can I try a shorter length?

Sure.

2. Here you are. They're on sale.

Thanks. Do you have a pair in green, too?

I'm sorry. We don't have that color in your size.

3. Look at me, Casey. I'm too short.

Not you. Me.

What are you talking about? We're not short.

But we're twins. We're the same height, and we're not short.

4. Stacey, what's the matter?

I didn't get the modeling job. They want a taller model. Casey, I need a better body.

5. That's crazy. You don't need a better body. You need a better job.

Yeah, right. That's what you say.

B. PAIR WORK Discuss. What is Stacey's problem? What does Casey think?

3 Grammar in Context

Making comparisons

Adjectives of comparison

To form the comparative, add **–er** to one-syllable adjectives.

short + **–er** = shorter
fast + **–er** = faster

Add **–r** if the adjective has one syllable and ends in an **e.**
nice + **–r** = nicer
large + **–r** = larger

Put **more** before most adjectives of two or more syllables.
more expensive   **more** attractive

For one-syllable and two-syllable adjectives that end in **y,** change the **y** to **i** and add **–er.**
pretty − **y** + **–ier** = prettier
easy − **y** + **–ier** = easier

Than links the two people or things you are comparing.
These jeans are shorter **than** those jeans.

Practice

A. **Look at the pictures. Think of other adjectives to describe the objects.**

B. **PAIR WORK** **Point to a picture. Compare. Take turns.**

   A: *The blue dress is more expensive than the red one.*
   B: *So, the red dress is cheaper than the blue one.*

LANGUAGE UP CLOSE

One replaces a noun that has already been mentioned.

This skirt looks better than the other **one.**

expensive

long

small

old

heavy

attractive

Pronunciation

C. **Listen to each sentence. Pay attention to the rising intonation.**

Which shirt, sir?
⇑

The green one next to those blue socks.
　　⇑　　　　　　　　　　⇑

D. **Listen and mark the rising intonation in each sentence.**

1. The yellow one, next to those white tennis shoes.

2. The gray one, next to those green shorts.

3. The beige one, next to those black suits.

4. The green one, next to those brown shoes.

5. The red one, next to those blue skirts.

E. **Listen again and repeat.**

Interact

F. **PAIR WORK** **Look at the picture. Work with a partner.
Take turns asking to try on clothes.**

A: *May I try on that T-shirt, please?*
B: *Which one?*
A: *The gray one, next to the green shorts.*

4 Grammar in Context

Explaining problems with clothes

too + adjective

A: Do you like this dress?
B: No, it's **too tight**.

A: Do you want to buy that hat?
B: No, it's **too big**.

Practice

A. PAIR WORK   Explain why you don't like or want these items. Use *small*, *big*, *long*, *short*, or *tight*.

Interact

B. PAIR WORK   Match the questions with the best answers. Practice them with a partner.

1. Do you want to play tennis this evening?   No, they're too long.

2. Do you want to read these books?   No, I'm too tired.

3. Do you like eating curry?   No, it's too unhealthy.

4. Are you going to buy concert tickets?   No, they're too expensive.

5. Do you want to eat at Big Burger?   No, it's too spicy.

C. PAIR WORK   Think of two more questions to ask your partner. Answer your partner's questions.

5 Vocabulary in Context

Describing clothes

loose,
relaxed fit

tight

Jeans were used as work clothes until 1935. That year they appeared for the first time in *Vogue,* a fashion magazine.

V-neck

round neck

long sleeve

short sleeve

Practice

A. Complete the dialogues. Use the vocabulary above.

A: Excuse me, can I help you?
B: I want to exchange these jeans.
A: What's the problem?
B: They don't fit. They're too _____.
      I can't walk in them.

A: I have to change this shirt.
B: Why? What's wrong with it?
A: Well, nothing. It's a nice shirt,
      but it has _____.
B: What's the problem?
A: I want to wear one with long sleeves.

B. PAIR WORK Practice the conversations.

Interact

C. PAIR WORK Write a conversation using another item of clothing. Practice it with a partner.

6 Listening in Context

A. Listen to the advertisement for Warner's Department Store, and write the number of the floor where you can find the following items.

men's shirts _____   shoes _____

ladies' clothes _____   T-shirts _____

B. Now listen again and circle the correct answer *True* (T) or *False* (F).

1. T/F   The sale is on the weekend.

2. T/F   All the shoes are on sale.

3. T/F   T-shirts are two for one.

4. T/F   The silk scarf is worth $100 dollars.

5. T/F   All scarves in the ladies' department are 50% off.

bargain = something sold at a much cheaper price than usual

7 Reading

Comparison shopping

Before you read

A. PAIR WORK Discuss shopping with a partner. Do you like shopping for clothes? What do you buy? Do you read advertisements before you buy?

While you read

B. Read the advertisement. How much is the difference between the prices of the two outfits?

outfit = a set of clothes

cashmere = fine, soft wool

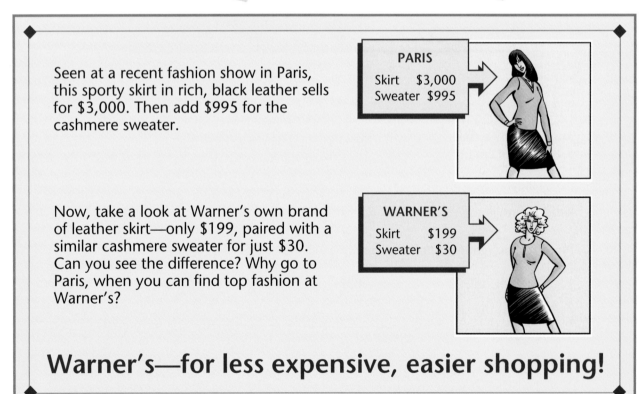

Seen at a recent fashion show in Paris, this sporty skirt in rich, black leather sells for $3,000. Then add $995 for the cashmere sweater.

PARIS
Skirt $3,000
Sweater $995

Now, take a look at Warner's own brand of leather skirt—only $199, paired with a similar cashmere sweater for just $30. Can you see the difference? Why go to Paris, when you can find top fashion at Warner's?

WARNER'S
Skirt $199
Sweater $30

Warner's—for less expensive, easier shopping!

After you read

C. PAIR WORK Do you compare prices when you buy clothes? Where do you usually shop? Do you think fashion is important? Discuss with a partner.

Writing

Advertisements

Before you write

A. PAIR WORK You are going to write an advertisement. Think of two similar products to compare. One should be better than the other. List adjectives you can use to compare them.

Example: *faster, cheaper, more attractive*

Write

B. Draw a picture of a product in each box. Then write the advertisement.

Product A	Product B

Advertisement

C. GROUP WORK Read your advertisement to your classmates. Which product would they buy?

A. You have $300 to spend. What are you going to buy?
Remember, you cannot spend more than $300.

shoes $50	coat $100	belt $25	scarf $25
dress $25	hat $25	sunglasses $25	skirt $50
jeans $50	sweater $100	T-shirt $25	tennis shoes $100
suit $100	boots $100	shorts $25	cap $15
pants $50	shirt $50	tie $25	jacket $50

B. **GROUP WORK**   Compare your choices with other students.
What did you choose? Why?

Practical Language

Identifying body parts and injuries

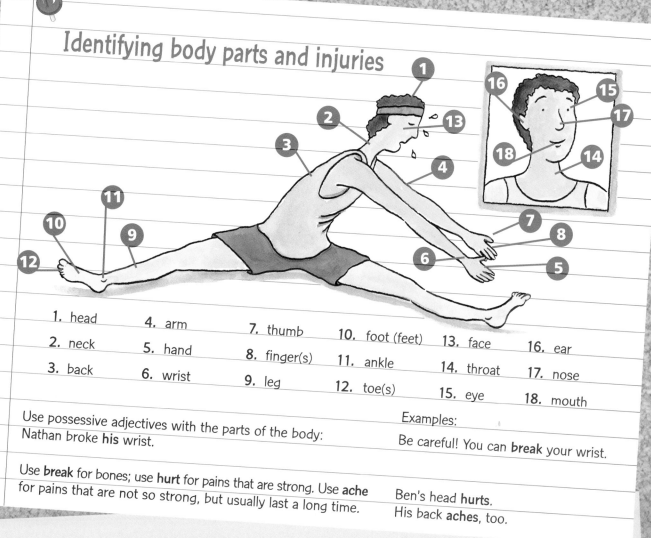

1. head
2. neck
3. back
4. arm
5. hand
6. wrist
7. thumb
8. finger(s)
9. leg
10. foot (feet)
11. ankle
12. toe(s)
13. face
14. throat
15. eye
16. ear
17. nose
18. mouth

Use possessive adjectives with the parts of the body:
Nathan broke **his** wrist.

Examples:
Be careful! You can **break** your wrist.

Use **break** for bones; use **hurt** for pains that are strong. Use **ache** for pains that are not so strong, but usually last a long time.

Ben's head **hurts**.
His back **aches**, too.

Numbers 120–99,000

120	one hundred (and) twenty	700	seven hundred
135	one hundred (and) thirty-five	800	eight hundred
140	one hundred (and) forty	900	nine hundred
189	one hundred (and) eighty-nine	1,000	one thousand
200	two hundred	1,500	one thousand five hundred or fifteen hundred
256	two hundred (and) fifty-six		
300	three hundred	6,000	six thousand
417	four hundred (and) seventeen	50,000	fifty thousand
500	five hundred	99,000	ninety-nine thousand
600	six hundred		

Describing the weather

To describe the weather, use:
noun + −y = adjective

For example:
cloud + −y = cloudy

What's the weather like?

A.

It's cloudy.

B.

It's rainy.

C.

It's windy.

D.

It's sunny.

E.

It's snowy.

More weather words

<u>hail:</u> frozen raindrops

<u>lightning:</u> a flash of light in the sky produced by atmospheric electricity

<u>thunder:</u> the sound that comes after lightning

<u>sleet:</u> a mixture of snow and rain

Note: We don't add −y to hail, thunder, or lightning to form adjectives.

How's the weather?

Think of five places in your country. Write a statement about each place telling what the weather is like in different months of the year.

Example: It's warm and sunny in Lima in January.

_____

_____

_____

_____

_____

I love the holidays.

Communication Goals	Grammar Goals	Vocabulary Goals
Describing objects	Nouns as adjectives	Materials
Talking about holidays	Superlatives	*It's made of silver.*
Talking about what things are made of		*Can I give you a hand?*
		It's out of my price range.

1 Warm Up

A. PAIR WORK Look at the pictures. What are these people thinking about? How are they going to spend their holidays?

LANGUAGE UP CLOSE

In the U.S., *the holidays* is the season from December to January 1st when many people celebrate Christmas, Hanukkah, Kwanza, and New Year's. At other times in the year, people celebrate other religious, national, and school holidays.

 B. Listen. What are they doing for the holidays? Write the number of the conversation next to correct picture.

What are you doing for the holidays?

I'm going to visit friends.

C. GROUP WORK Ask your classmates about their holidays.

I bought the most beautiful silver necklace.

A. Listen and practice.

1.

Hi Stacey. Are you going home? Can I help you with those bags?

I can give you a hand, too.

Thanks. That would be great. You're the best neighbors.

2.

How's your holiday shopping going?

Fine. I bought the most beautiful necklace for my mother.

Let me help you with those bags.

3.

Oops!

What's it made of?

Silver. It's from Mexico. Now I just need a present for Casey.

4.

What does Casey want? I'd like to get her a small gift.

She likes gold jewelry . . .

Oh. That's a little out of my price range.

5.

Can I give you a hand with the rest of those bags?

Thanks, Ken! Mike, I'm sure Casey would like whatever you get her. You're both the greatest!

B. Match the expression to its meaning.

_____ It's out of my price range.

_____ Can I give you a hand?

a. Can I help you with something?
b. That's too much money for me to pay.

3 Grammar in Context

Describing objects

Nouns as adjectives

A noun used as an adjective goes before the noun it modifies.

Stacey bought a necklace.   It's made of **silver.**   She bought a **silver** necklace.
Casey wants a wallet.   It's made of **leather.**   She wants a **leather** wallet.

silver necklace

leather wallet

gold earrings

silk scarf

Practice

A. Fill in the blanks with words from the boxes. Share your answers with a partner.

gold	leather	silk	coins	wallet	scarf
silver	wool	cotton	earrings	blouse	coat

1. It's made of _____.   It's for the neck or head.
   It's a _____ _____.

2. They're made of _____.   They're expensive.
   They're _____ _____.

3. It's made of _____.   It holds your money.
   It's a _____ _____.

4. They're made of _____.   People collect them.
   They're _____ _____.

5. It's made of _____.   It keeps you warm.
   It's a _____ _____.

6. It's made of _____.   It goes with a skirt or pants.
   It's a _____ _____.

Pronunciation

B. Listen to the words and repeat them.

C. PAIR WORK Look at the list of words as you listen again. What difference do you hear between the two words? Discuss with a partner.

D. Listen to the new list of words. Check the word you hear.

_____ made		_____ mad	
_____ Cate		_____ cat	
_____ rate		_____ rat	
_____ hate		_____ hat	
_____ plane		_____ plan	
_____ cane		_____ can	
_____ mane		_____ man	

Some articles of clothing are made of more than one material: cotton and polyester, nylon and lycra.

Interact

E. GROUP WORK Ask your classmates what their clothes are made of.

A: *What is your shirt made of?*
B: *It's made of cotton and polyester.*

4 Grammar in Context

Talking about holidays

L ANGUAGE UP CLOSE

Some adjectives have irregular comparative and superlative forms.

good   better   best

Superlatives		
Adjectives with one syllable		
The	adjective + **–est**	noun
The	greatest	movie
The	saddest	experience
Adjectives with more than one syllable		
The	**most** + adjective	noun
The	most exciting	trip
The	most wonderful	holiday

A: What did you do over the holidays?
B: I had the **most wonderful** time. I saw the **best** movie and took the **most exciting** trip. It was the **greatest** experience.

Listening

A. **Listen. Check the things the people did on their vacation.**

Best	Worst
_____ I saw the most beautiful sunset.	_____ We had the worst weather.
_____ I had the most wonderful holiday.	_____ I had the most terrible accident.
_____ I went to the best party.	_____ I was the most frightened.
_____ I visited the most interesting museum.	_____ I went to the most boring party.
_____ I saw the most exciting movie.	_____ I had the most dangerous experience.
_____ I ate the most delicious food.	_____ I went to the worst play.

B. **PAIR WORK** **Compare your answers with your partner.**

Practice

C. **Complete the sentences with adjectives of your choice.**

1. I saw the _____ movie Saturday night.

2. I went to the _____ party last weekend.

3. I had the _____ holiday this summer.

4. I ate the _____ food while I was on vacation.

5. We had the _____ weather on our trip.

LANGUAGE **UP CLOSE**

Always use *the* or a possessive pronoun before superlative adjectives.

That is **the** best dessert. Pat is **my** best friend.

D. **PAIR WORK** **Share your answers with a partner.**

Interact

E. **GROUP WORK** **Ask your classmates about the best or worst part of their most recent holiday. Write their answers in the chart below.**

Classmate	Best	Worst
Anna	went to the most interesting museum	had the worst food

F. **GROUP WORK** **Share your answers with the whole group.**

Example: *I talked to Anna. She went to the most interesting museum, but she ate the worst food.*

Talking about what things are made of

cotton   silk   wool   leather

A:	What's this blouse		?
B:	It's		silk.
A:	Is the skirt	made of	silk, too?
B:	No, it isn't. It's		cotton.

Practice

A. Match the item with the material.

1. —

2. —

a. plastic
b. denim
c. silver
d. cotton
e. wool

3. —

4. —

5. —

 B. Listen to check your answers.

Interact

C. PAIR WORK Ask and answer questions about the items in the pictures on page 50.

A: *What are blue jeans **made of**?*
B: *They're **made of** denim.*

Other materials: wood, plastic, metal, steel, iron, cement

D. GROUP WORK Look at the list of classroom objects below. Which of these items are in your classroom? Take turns. Name an item and say what it is made of.

Example: *The chair is made of wood.*

chair	table	desk	board	bookshelf	map
ruler	locker	poster	clock	cabinet	lamp

6 Listening in Context

A. Listen to the radio announcement. Answer the questions below.

1. What kind of announcement is it?   news   weather   advertisement

2. Where does it tell you to go? _____

3. Why is this place special? _____

4. Is this type of announcement common on your local radio stations? _____

B. Listen again. Fill in the blanks with the correct adjectives.

1. the _____ gifts
2. the _____ prices
3. the _____ variety of clothing
4. the _____ toys and games
5. the _____ selection of gold jewelry
6. the _____ designer party clothes

New Year's celebrations

Before you read

A. PAIR WORK Discuss with a partner what you do to celebrate New Year's.

While you read

B. Underline the dishes and objects. Circle what they are made of.

Different cultures have different ways to celebrate the New Year. Many cultures celebrate with special dishes and objects. In China, people prepare traditional food to share with friends and family. On New Year's Day, Chinese families eat a dish called *jai*. It is made of Chinese vegetables like ginkgo nuts, lotus seeds, black moss seaweed, and bamboo shoots. Each of the vegetables has a special meaning. The Chinese also traditionally celebrate the New Year with fireworks. They first used them as early as the eighth century A.D. Fireworks are made of materials like sulfur, charcoal, and saltpeter (also known as potassium nitrate).

In Mexico, a traditional New Year's dish is *tamales*. Tamales are made from corn meal, meat, or vegetables in a chili sauce and are wrapped in banana leaves. They are cooked for a long time in a steamer. People of all ages also like to break *piñatas* at New Year's. Piñatas are made of colored crepe paper and *papier mâché*. They have a large clay pot with candy and fruit inside. To get at the sweets in the pot, everyone tries to break the piñata.

After you read

C. Fill in the chart with the information you read. Check your answers with a partner.

	China	**Mexico**
Dish: Made of:	Jai gingko nuts, lotus seeds, black moss seaweed, bamboo shoots	
Object: Made of:		

The worst vacation

Before you write

A. PAIR WORK Make a list of things that happened on your worst vacation. Discuss your list with your partner.

Write

B. Write to your friend about your worst vacation. What made it a bad vacation?

We had the worst vacation. We . . .

C. GROUP WORK. Read your comments to your classmates.

A. PAIR WORK   Think of traditional dishes in your country, city, or region. Make a list.

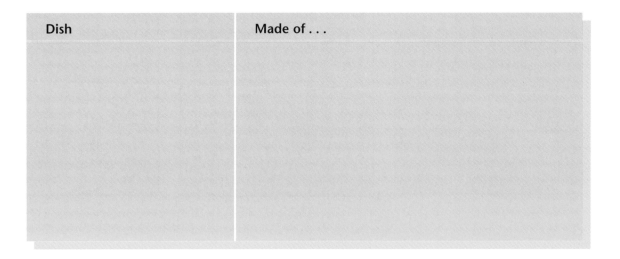

Dish	Made of . . .

B. GROUP WORK   Divide into two teams. Each team will think of traditional holiday dishes. One team will describe to the other team what one of the dishes is made of. The other team guesses the name of the dish. If they guess correctly, they win one point. If they guess incorrectly, the other team gets a point. At the end, the team with the most points wins.

We should take a vacation.

Communication Goals	Grammar Goals	Vocabulary Goals
Talking about possibility	Modals: *could, should, will, have to*	Tourist attractions
Making weather predictions	Adjectives: *far, high, deep, long*	Numbers
Making suggestions for vacation plans		*It should rain tomorrow.*
Asking about tourist attractions		*How far is it?*
		How long will it take?

1 Warm Up

A. PAIR WORK Look at the photos. Which place would you like to visit on your next vacation? Discuss.

B. Listen to a customer at a travel agency trying to decide on the right vacation spot. Where do you think the customer will go? What questions do you think the customer will ask?

Puerto Rico

Switzerland

India

Mexico

Kenya

Japan

2 Conversation

We should visit my mother.

A. Listen and practice.

It's the weekend. Susan, Kevin, and Andy are rollerblading on Santa Monica Beach.

1.

What's wrong, Susan? Are you tired?

Yes. You know, we're working too hard. We should take a vacation.

2.

Why don't we drive to Arizona and visit the Grand Canyon? We could also take a boat ride on the Colorado River.

3.

How far is it from Los Angeles to the Grand Canyon?

I'm not sure. I think its about 450 miles.

By car? That's too far!

4.

Why don't we go to Hawaii and visit my mother there? Families should be together over the holidays.

Yeah, and I could go snorkeling.

Come on! It'll be a second honeymoon for us.

5.

Yeah, Dad. It'll be a second honeymoon.

OK. We'll go to Hawaii.

B. Answer the following questions.

1. Where does Kevin want to go?
2. What does he want to do there?
3. Why doesn't Andy want to go?
4. Where do Susan and Andy want to go?
5. Where are they going to go on vacation?

3 Grammar in Context

Asking for and making suggestions

Questions with modals	Suggestions with modals
Where **should** they go on vacation?	They **could** go to Kenya.
What **should** I take with me to the mountains?	You **should** take your hiking boots.
When **should** I make reservations for the flight?	You **have to** make reservations soon.
How **should** we go to Toronto?	We **can** fly there. Driving takes too long.

Practice

A. PAIR WORK Take turns asking about and suggesting places to visit and things to see.

pyramid

temple

nightlife

mountain

wildlife park

Example: Egypt / interesting pyramids

A: *Where should I go on vacation?*
B: *You could go to Egypt.*
A: *Which places should I visit?*
B: *You should go to the pyramids. They're so interesting.*

1. Thailand / wonderful temples
2. Brazil / exciting nightlife
3. France / interesting museums
4. Switzerland / beautiful mountains
5. Kenya / incredible wildlife parks

> I have no plans for next weekend.

> You could go to _____.

B. GROUP WORK Look at the photos on page 55. Take turns asking about each place and interesting things to do there. Ask other questions about the trip.

Interact

C. GROUP WORK Take turns asking for and making suggestions about where to go near your town or city and what to do, see, and eat there.

D. Make a list of the places your group suggests. Together write a new question and a suggestion about each place.

> You should see _____.

> And you have to eat _____.

4 Grammar in Context

Talking about possibility

Modals		
It **could** snow this weekend.	50%	Possible
It **should** be clear tomorrow.	75%	Likely
It **will** be a hot summer.	100%	Certain

Practice

A. Read the conversations carefully. Fill in the blanks using *could*, *should*, or *will*.

Jason: Let's go to the beach tomorrow!

Brad: I don't know. It _____ be rainy. Look at the clouds outside

Jason: I don't think it's going to rain. The weather report said it _____ be sunny.

Brad: All right then, let's go to the beach!

Jason: Hey, do you think Casey and Stacey _____ want to come too?

Casey: How'd it go, Stacey? Did you get the job?

Stacey: Well, I'm not sure. I _____ get it.

Casey: I'm sure you _____ get the job.

Stacey: They asked me to come back tomorrow. I really _____ get it.

B. PAIR WORK Practice the conversations above.

CULTURE
UP CLOSE

Many people enjoy vacations with lots of outdoor activities. The Trans Canada Trail, where tourists can hike, bicycle, or ski, is 16,000 km long.

C. Look at tomorrow's weather map and decide if the following statements are true or false.

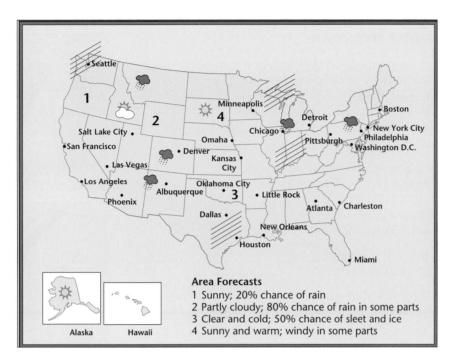

Area Forecasts
1 Sunny; 20% chance of rain
2 Partly cloudy; 80% chance of rain in some parts
3 Clear and cold; 50% chance of sleet and ice
4 Sunny and warm; windy in some parts

1. It will be sunny in Denver tomorrow.
2. It should be very cold in Houston.
3. It could be warm in Anchorage.
4. It will be sunny and windy in Chicago.
5. It should rain in Albuquerque.

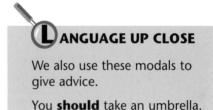

LANGUAGE UP CLOSE

We also use these modals to give advice.

You **should** take an umbrella.

Interact

D. PAIR WORK Take turns giving your partner advice on what to wear in the different cities on the map. Use the weather predictions from the map.

What will the weather be like in Little Rock?

It could be very hot. You should take summer clothes.

5 Vocabulary in Context

Asking about tourist attractions

Hannah: **How far is it to** the wildlife park?
Steve: It's about 50 miles.
Hannah: **How long will it take to get there?**
Steve: About an hour.

Andy: **How high is** that mountain?
Guide: It's a volcano. It's about 2,500 meters.
Andy: **How many feet is that?**
Guide: It's about 8,200 feet.
Andy: **How deep is** the crater?
Guide: It's about 350 feet deep.

Susan: **How old is** this temple?
Guide: It's about 400 years old.

Andy: **How long is** this beach?
Kevin: I'm not sure, but it's probably 10 miles long.

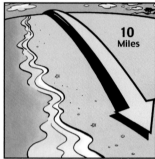

 A. Listen to the conversations. Practice them with your partner.

CULTURE
UP CLOSE

Height can be measured either in **meters** or **feet**, distance in **kilometers** or **miles**, and weight in **kilograms** or **pounds**. The U.S. normally uses feet, miles, and pounds. Most other countries in the world use the metric system. For example, 2,500 m = 8,200 ft.

Pronunciation

B. Pronounce these numbers. The larger dots show where to emphasize when pronouncing numbers.

1. 123   one hundred twenty-three

2. 200   two hundred

3. 409   four hundred nine

4. 1,000   one thousand

5. 2,450   two thousand four hundred fifty

6. 17,000   seventeen thousand

7. 839   eight hundred thirty-nine

Practice

C. PAIR WORK Student A, use the chart below. Student B, turn to page 127. Complete the missing information in your chart by asking your partner questions.

Number of miles between some U.S. cities			
From	**To Chicago**	**To Kansas City**	**To New York**
Boston	994	1,391	
Los Angeles	2,054		
Seattle			2,815
Washington, D.C.	671		233

 Interact

D. GROUP WORK Share some information about the distance between cities and about the height, length, and age of geographical landmarks in your region or country. How much do you know?

How far is it from Osaka to Tokyo?

It's about 400 kilometers.

And how tall is the Tokyo Tower?

 # 6 Listening in Context

A. Listen and decide. When will be the best time for Ken to visit his friend in Chicago next week? Explain your answer.

B. Listen again. Write a weather prediction for Chicago for each day in the chart below. Use *could*, *should*, and *will*.

Monday	Tuesday	Wednesday	Thursday	Friday	Saturday	Sunday
					The weather should be nice.	

7 Reading

Visting Hawaii Volcanoes National Park

Before you read

A. PAIR WORK Discuss these questions with a partner.

1. Do you like to travel?

2. Do you read travel brochures or visit travel websites?

3. What kind of information can you find in travel brochures or on travel websites? Make a list.

Hawaii Volcanoes National Park

About the Park
The six islands that make up the state of Hawaii, Kauai, Oahu, Maui, Molokai, Lanai, and Hawaii were formed through millions of years of volcanic activity.
　The Hawaii Volcanoes National Park, on the island of Hawaii (also known as the Big Island), has two active volcanoes. The biggest is Mauna Loa, which means "Long Mountain." Mauna Loa is the world's most massive volcano. Mauna Loa is 13,677 feet (4.17 km) above sea level.
　Kilauea is next to Mauna Loa and it is the most active volcano in the world. From some areas in the park, you can see volcanic activity such as lava flows and eruptions.

When to Visit
The park is open 24 hours a day year round. There are no plants or trees on the lava fields and no protection from the sun, so you must bring sunscreen.

How to Get There
The best way to get to the park is to take Highway 11. From the airport at Hilo, Highway 11 will take you southward across the eastern part of the island.

Things to See
There are many guided walks and hikes around the park. You can also walk on trails without a guide to direct you. The Kilauea Visitor Center is a quarter mile (402 m) from the park entrance. There, you can learn about the island's geological, natural, and cultural history.
　The center is open from 7:45 a.m. to 5:00 p.m. You must check weather conditions and volcanic activity before hiking alone. If conditions permit, you can drive down Chain of Craters Road to see lava flowing into the ocean.

Econotes
Do not climb on, collect, or alter any rocks or rock structures, including *heiau* (ancient temples) and petroglyphs. Also, do not feed the endangered *nene*, Hawaii's state bird.

For More Information
Contact the Park Superintendent, P.O. Box 52, Hawaii National Park, Hilo, HI 96718; 967-7311.

While you read

B. Circle the items from your list that you find in this travel brochure.

After you read

C. Look back at the reading. Find words that mean the same as the ones below.

1. _____ change

2. _____ allow

3. _____ very large

D. Answer the following questions.

1. On which island is Hawaii Volcanoes National Park?

2. Name two active volcanoes on the island.

3. What are the two types of volcanic activity mentioned in the reading?

4. What is the Hawaiian word for ancient temple?

5. What is the name of Hawaii's state bird?

8 Writing

What should I see there?

Before you write

A. What is your country famous for? Make a list of special tourist attractions.

Write

B. Answer the questions below in complete sentences. Then copy them into paragraph form to produce a travel brochure for your country or region.

1. Where is your country located?

2. What geographical attraction is it famous for?

3. How can you travel to this place?

4. What can you do there?

5. What can you see there?

6. How can you find out more information about it?

9 Putting It Together

A. Think of a country, city, or popular tourist spot. Do not tell anyone what it is.

B. **GROUP WORK** Take turns. Your classmates will ask questions to guess the place. Each person may ask one question, until someone guesses the place. The person who guesses will be asked questions next.

Casey! Watch out!

Communication Goals	Grammar Goals	Vocabulary Goals
Talking about future plans and schedules Giving warnings Talking about frequency Giving advice	Present progressive with future meaning Questions with *how often* Adverbs: *once, twice, every*	Housework *What about you?* *Have fun!* *Watch out!*

1 Warm Up

A. Label the pictures of housework activities using the vocabulary in the box.

doing laundry	dusting
vacuuming	cooking
shopping	ironing

_____   _____   _____

chore = a job that must be done.

_____   _____   _____

B. PAIR WORK Discuss. Do you do housework? What do you do?

 C. Listen to Karen and Nathan talking about housework. Circle the activities you hear.

shopping   cleaning the bathroom   ironing   doing laundry   cooking

2 Conversation

What are you doing today?

A. Look at the story and listen.

1.
What are you doing today?

We're going shopping. What about you?

I'm painting Jason's living room.

Well, have fun.

2.
Well, what do you think? Should we paint the room green?

Hmmm. I think we should paint it blue.

3.
Hey, Casey, are we going to a movie later?

No, let's stay home and finish painting.

4.
Casey! Watch out!

Oops!

5.
You know, I don't think I like this blue after all.

B. Discuss. What is everyone going to do today? What does Jason want to do? What happens to Casey?

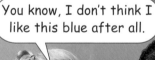

3 Grammar in Context

Talking about future plans

be verb + -ing with future meaning

You can use **am / is / are** + **verb** + **-ing** (present progressive) for the future when you are talking about plans and activities. You also have to mention the future time when the activity will take place.

A: What are you doing on Sunday?

B: I'm painting my room.

A: What's Nathan doing on the weekend?

B: He's helping Karen with the housework.

Practice

A. Look at Annie and Ben's schedules for the next week.

Ben
Monday – Finish chapter four.
Tuesday – Take car for service.
Wednesday – Buy computer software.
Thursday – Go to movies with Annie.
Friday – clean Sebastian's cage.
Saturday – Go shopping.
Sunday – cook meal for friends.

Annie
Monday – Go to grocery store.
Tuesday – Clean pool.
Wednesday – Play tennis with Karen.
Thursday – Go to the movies.
Friday – Send out rent receipts.
Saturday – Get new sneakers.
Sunday – Visit clare.

B. PAIR WORK Take turns. Ask and answer questions about their plans.

Example: **A:** *What's Ben doing on Sunday?*

   B: *He's cooking a meal.*

Interact

C. On a piece of paper, list your plans for next week.

D. PAIR WORK Take turns asking and answering questions about your plans.

Pronunciation

E. Listen to the stressed words.

    •   •   •
1. Casey! Watch out!

    •   •   •
2. Stacey! Be careful!

    •   •   •   •
3. Jason! Look behind you!

    •   •   •
4. Andy! Don't run!

    •   •   •
5. Brad! Slow down!

F. Listen again and repeat.

G. Match each picture with a warning.

> ## LANGUAGE UP CLOSE
>
> When you give a warning, use the base form of the verb.
>
> Watch out!

Interact

H. GROUP WORK Take turns acting out or describing a dangerous action while the others call out a warning.

4 Grammar in Context

Talking about frequency

LANGUAGE UP CLOSE

Other frequency expressions:
every other day / week / month
every few days / weeks / months
every now and then

Questions with *How often...?*

How often	do	you	clean the house?
	does	he/she	
I	clean the house	once a twice a three times a every	day. week. month.
He/She	cleans the house		

Practice

A. **PAIR WORK** Ask and answer questions about Bob's schedule.

Windcrest High School Class Schedule				Bob Riley	
Time	Monday	Tuesday	Wednesday	Thursday	Friday
8:10 AM	English	English	English	English	English
9:00 AM	Math	Math	Math	Math	Math
9:50 AM	study period	Art	study period	Art	study period
10:40 AM	Chemistry	Chemistry	Chemistry	Chemistry	Chemistry
11:30 AM	History	History	History	History	History
12:20 PM	lunch	lunch	lunch	lunch	lunch
1:10 PM	French	French	French	French	French
2:00 PM	soccer practice	basketball practice	basketball practice	soccer practice	soccer practice

Example: **A:** *How often does Bob have math class?*
            B: *Five times a week—on Monday, Tuesday, Wednesday, Thursday, and Friday.*

CULTURE UP CLOSE

The American school system has 12 grades, plus kindergarten. In most places, students go to elementary school, middle (or junior high) school, and high school

 **Interact**

B. PAIR WORK Write a list of things you do regularly; for example, *go to the movies, go for a run, study math, cook dinner, visit your grandparents.* Exchange lists with another student, and ask each other how often you do each activity.

5 Vocabulary in Context

Housework

wash the dishes

dry the dishes

rake the leaves

vacuum the carpet

water the plants

mow the lawn

Practice

A. Complete the conversations. Use words from the activities above.

1. Annie: Thanks for helping me out, Stacey. Which do you prefer, to wash or _____ the dishes?

   Stacey: Either one is okay with me. After this do you want me to _____ the plants?

2. Susan: Andy, hurry up and _____ the lawn so we can go to the movies this afternoon.

   Andy: Mom, do I have to _____ the leaves too?

B. PAIR WORK Practice the conversations with a partner.

Interact

C. Write and practice your own conversations using some of the vocabulary above.

6 Listening in Context

A. Listen to Lucy's "Can I Help You?" live radio show. Answer the questions.

1. What is Stephanie's problem?
2. What does Lucy think she should do?

B. Listen again and answer the true / false questions.

1. T/F   Nicole and Stephanie work long hours.

2. T/F   They share the housework.

3. T/F   Stephanie goes out with her boyfriend on the weekends.

4. T/F   Lucy thinks Stephanie should go out next weekend.

5. T/F   Lucy thinks Stephanie should do more housework.

C. PAIR WORK   Do you agree with Lucy's advice? What do you think Nicole and Stephanie are going to say after the weekend?

Interact

D. PAIR WORK   Write a conversation between Stephanie and Nicole on Monday morning. Practice it with your partner.

CULTURE UP CLOSE

The U.S. Consumer Product Safety Commission reports an annual estimate of injuries and accidents related to household items. The top 5 were:

Products	Number of injuries
Glass doors and window panels	216,193
Workshop manual tools	125,780
Exercise equipment	95,127
Lawnmowers	85,202
Cooking ranges and ovens	53,401

7 Reading

Housework is good for you.

Before you read

A. GROUP WORK Discuss these questions with your classmates.

1. Do you ever feel stressed?
2. What can you do to feel better?

Men spend 10 hours per week doing household chores. Women spend 17.5 hours per week.

While you read

B. Read the magazine article. Underline all the words about housework.

Does Housework Keep You Sane?

It seems impossible, but now experts are praising housework.

"Simple household chores such as ironing or mowing the lawn can offer drug-free ways of coping with stress,"
(5) says a leading New York psychologist. She advises her clients to turn their daily chores into a kind of therapy.

"While washing the windows," she tells them, "imagine that you are wiping away all the little things in life that are bothering you. While ironing, imagine you are smoothing
(10) out the problems of your life." She also says that housework can bring a sense of satisfaction to your life.

Work these days can be very difficult and stressful, so doing something simple, even if it is only washing dirty dishes, can give you a feeling of accomplishment, as well
(15) as help you to relax.

praise = to say something good

cope = to manage

After you read

C. GROUP WORK Do you agree with the psychologist's ideas? What other ways are there to cope with stress? Discuss your ideas with your classmates.

D. Pronouns are used so the author doesn't have to repeat names in every sentence. Look back at the article and write the noun that these pronouns replace.

1. *she* in line 5 _____

2. *them* in line 7 _____

3. *it* in line 13 _____

8 Writing

Writing a letter

Before you write

A. PAIR WORK Discuss different household problems that people might have.

Write

B. Choose one of the problems. Then write a letter to ask for advice about it.

> Dear Lucy,
> I have a problem,
>
>
>
>
>
>   Yours truly,

C. PAIR WORK Read your letter to a classmate. Can your partner give some good advice to help you?

9 Putting It Together

A. GROUP WORK Interview some people in your class.
Ask them how often they do different things. Fill in the chart.

How often do you go to the movies?

Twice a month.

name	go grocery shopping	clean your room	wash the dishes	vacuum the carpets	iron your clothes	study English

B. GROUP WORK Share your answers with other
classmates. Who does housework most often?
Who studies English most often? What about
the least often?

Stay TUNED

Where will Andy be meeting Elvis?

I made my reservation two weeks ago.

Communication Goals	Grammar Goals	Vocabulary Goals
Asking about travel	Information questions	Travel
Expressing length of time	Time expressions + *ago*	*I'm sorry—my mistake.*
Making and responding to polite requests	Modal *could*	*How long ago did you go?*
		Could you help me?

1 Warm Up

A. Listen to the conversations. Write the number of the conversation on the correct line.

B. PAIR WORK Compare your answers with your partner. Explain why you answered the way you did.

2 Conversation

Can I have a window seat, please?

Kevin is going to a medical convention in Las Vegas.

A. Listen and practice.

1.

Good morning, sir. Where are you traveling today?

Las Vegas.

Could I see your ticket, please?

2.

I'm sorry. I don't see your name on this flight.

But I made my reservation two weeks ago.

Oh, here it is. I'm sorry—my mistake.

Could I have a window and an aisle seat?

3.

How many bags do you have?

Just these two.

4.

All right, sir. Your seat numbers are 20A and 20B. Your flight begins boarding at Gate 18 at 2:15. Here are your boarding passes.

5.

Dad, why did you get two seats?

Happy Birthday Andy! I'm taking you to Las Vegas with me.

B. Answer the following questions.

1. Why is Kevin going to Las Vegas?
2. Why is Andy going to Las Vegas?

3 Grammar in Context

Asking about travel

Information questions

How long	did	you		stay	at your grandmother's house?
	did	Elena			in Japan?
Who	did	Susan		visit	last year?
	did	your parents			on their trip?
When	did	you		go	to Korea?
	did	Michael			to Europe?

Practice

A. PAIR WORK Ask your partner about the people in the chart below.

Example: **A:** *Who did Susan visit in 1999?*
B: *She visited her father.*
A: *How long did she stay?*
B: *For three weeks.*

Who	When	People visited	Length of visit
Susan	1999	her father	three weeks
The Wongs	2000	their cousins	ten days
Adela	last month	Anna Barnes	one day
Joseph and his mother	1998	his uncle Paul	three weeks
Howard	last weekend	his wife's parents	two days
Elizabeth and Sarah	1982	Mexico	two weeks

Interact

B. PAIR WORK Talk to your partner about past trips. Ask
questions with *Who did . . . ?*, *What did. . . ?*, *How long did. . . ?*,
and *Where did?*

Example: **A:** *Where did you go on your last vacation?*
B: *I went to Singapore to visit my friend.*

4 Grammar in Context

Expressing length of time

Questions and answers with *when* and *how long ago*					
How long ago		you	see that movie?	Three months	
	did	Mr. Wilson	visit Rome?	Two years	ago.
When		dinosaurs	live on the Earth?	Thousands of years	

Practice

A. PAIR WORK Ask your partner questions about the communication time line.

Example: **A:** *How long ago did Samuel Morse invent the telegraph?*
B: *About 200 years ago.*

about = approximately

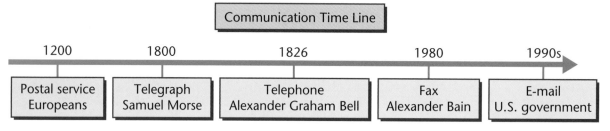

Communication Time Line

1200	1800	1826	1980	1990s
Postal service Europeans	Telegraph Samuel Morse	Telephone Alexander Graham Bell	Fax Alexander Bain	E-mail U.S. government

Interact

B. GROUP WORK Ask your classmates about famous events in the history of your country or city.

C. Make your own timeline with five things you did over the past few months or years. Do not write the dates.

D. PAIR WORK Exchange papers, and ask your partner questions to find out the dates on his or her timeline.

CULTURE
UP CLOSE

The total estimated time of flight delays in Europe due to computer delays and strikes is calculated at 57 years.

5 Vocabulary in Context

Making and responding to polite requests

Could I see your **ticket** please?

Of course.

Could you show me your **passport**, please?

Yes, here it is.

Could you help me with my **luggage?**

Sure.

Could you help me? I can't find my **bag/suitcase.**

Certainly. Don't worry.

Could you give me my **seat number?**

The **agent** at the check-in counter will give it to you.

Could you tell me where to **board** my plane?

Yes, your plane leaves from **gate** 12.

Practice

A. Complete the conversations with one of the words or expressions above.

1. **A:** Do you have a lot of _____ ?
   B: No, I just have these two bags.
2. **A:** Excuse me. Where do I board Flight 407 for Miami?
   B: At _____ 43.
3. **A:** What's your _____ ?
   B: 15A. It's a window seat.
4. **A:** Could you tell me where I can buy a _____ ?
   B: Over there at the first counter.
5. **A:** Do I have to show my passport at the first counter?
   B: I'm not sure. Why don't you ask the _____ ?

> **L**ANGUAGE UP CLOSE
>
> Use *Could I . . .?* when you are asking for something.
>
> Use *Could you . . .?* when you want someone to do something for you.

Listening

B. Listen to the conversations. Check *affirmative* or *negative* according to the response you hear to each question.

1. _____ affirmative   _____ negative
2. _____ affirmative   _____ negative
3. _____ affirmative   _____ negative
4. _____ affirmative   _____ negative
5. _____ affirmative   _____ negative

C. PAIR WORK Ask your partner questions using the travel vocabulary on page 79.

 Interact

D. PAIR WORK Take turns asking questions and responding affirmatively or negatively to polite requests.

1. You work in security at the airport. You want to look inside a traveler's suitcase. What do you say to the traveler?

2. You are at the train station. You don't know where to buy your ticket. What do you say to the guard at the door?

3. You are on a plane. You want to read a newspaper on the flight. What do you say to the attendant?

4. You are at the ticket counter. You want to change the time of your flight to Seattle from morning to afternoon. What do you say to the agent?

5. You are on the plane. You would like to sit in the window seat. What do you say to the person next to you?

A. Listen and fill in the chart with the missing information.

roller skates   miniskirt   sneakers

umbrella   rollercoaster   television

When	Who	What
	Jonas Hanway	
	Joseph Merlin	invented roller skates
mid 1800s	Europeans and Americans	had rollercoasters in amusement parks
	The U.S. Rubber Company	
1967	Mary Quant	
	Philo T. Farnsworth	

B. PAIR WORK Use the finished chart to ask and answer questions about things that happened in the past.

Example:
A: *When did Mary Quant invent the miniskirt?* OR *How long ago did Mary Quant create the miniskirt?*
B: *In 1967. That was _____ years ago.*

7 Reading

Travel test

Before you read

A. PAIR WORK Discuss. How long is your vacation? Do you always travel on your vacation?

While you read

B. Read the questions, and check your answers. Then use your score to find out what kind of traveler you are.

What kind of traveler are you?

1. How long do you usually go on vacation?
____ a. Less than a week.
____ b. One to two weeks.
____ c. More than two weeks.

2. Do you prefer to . . .
____ a. go shopping and sightseeing?
____ b. relax by the beach and swim?
____ c. enjoy outdoor activities like hiking and other sports?

3. What time of year do you usually go on vacation?
____ a. Around national holidays.
____ b. In summer.
____ c. Anytime. It doesn't matter.

4. Who do you usually go with?
____ a. Family.
____ b. Friends.
____ c. Alone.

5. How much luggage do you take?
____ a. One or two suitcases.
____ b. More than two suitcases.
____ c. One small bag or backpack.

Now add up your score:
For every *a* answer, 1 point.
For every *b* answer, 2 points.
For every *c* answer, 4 points.

Use your total score to find out what type of traveler you are below.

9 or less: You are a *Reluctant Traveler*. You are a busy person who really doesn't like to slow down. You only take short breaks, usually when there is a national holiday. You prefer traveling to cities, and you like to stay in nice hotels. You often spend time with your family on vacation.

10 to 15: You are a *Comfort Traveler*. All you want to do is put your worries behind you. In the summer, you love to take a few weeks off, relax, and catch up with friends. You like to try new things, and after a couple of days lazing around, you're usually ready for more active pursuits.

16 and above: You are an *Intrepid Traveler*. You love to explore new places and see new things. You like to travel overseas, with friends, or on your own. You love to have new experiences and adventures in out-of-the-way places. You are happy visiting cities, jungles, or small islands, but package tours aren't for you.

After you read

C. GROUP WORK Do you agree with the results of the test? Why or why not? Share your opinions with your classmates.

8 Writing

A travel journal

Before you write

A. Make a list of things you like to do when you travel. Divide the items into groups using a mind map like the one on the right.

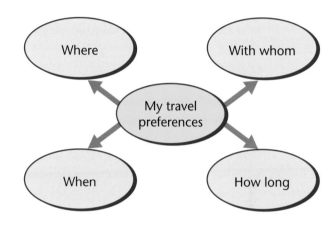

Write

B. Use the above information to write a report about how you like to travel.

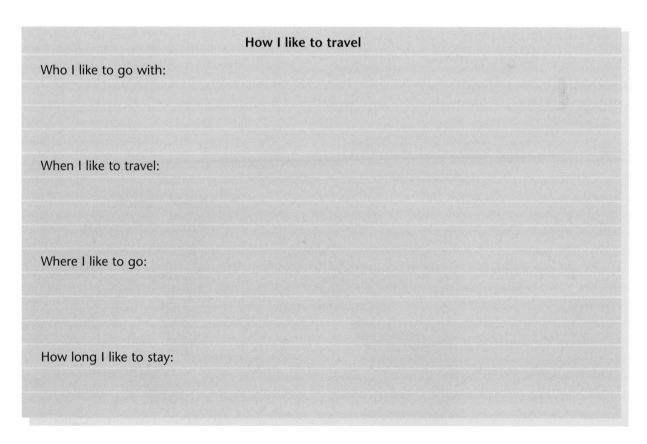

How I like to travel

Who I like to go with:

When I like to travel:

Where I like to go:

How long I like to stay:

C. GROUP WORK Share your report with your classmates.

9 Putting It Together

A. GROUP WORK Ask your classmates questions about
the way they like to travel.

Example:
A: *How do you like to travel?*
B: *I like to travel by bus.*

B. Mark an X in the correct column for each answer
you hear from your classmates.

Bus	Train	Car	Airplane	Other

C. GROUP WORK Use the chart to find your group's
favorite way to travel.

Stay **TUNED**

Who's this with
Phil Chen?

Practical Language

Getting a job

Phil Chen is an **applicant** for a job as a graphic designer. He called the personnel office to make an **appointment** for an **interview**. He sent his **resume** before the interview. The personnel manager **interviewed** Phil today.

Complete the conversation using one of these words: education, receptionist, job ad, interview, appointment, experience, applicants.

Casey: How was the interview, Stacey?

Stacey: It was OK, but there are a lot of _____.

Casey: Don't worry about it, Stacey. Look! Did you see this _____ for an executive assistant?

Stacey: Yes, I did.

Casey: Are you going to make a/an _____ for a/an _____ for this job, too?

Stacey: I don't think so. I don't have the right kind of _____.

Casey: But you have a good _____, and you can type.

Stacey: That's true. But and I don't have any real office experience.

Casey: Didn't you work in an office one summer at that Beverly Hills hotel?

Stacey: Well, yes. But I was a _____.

Casey: OK, now I remember.

Two-word verbs

A verb and a preposition can be combined to form a two-word verb.
A two-word verb is a verb a preposition that together have a
new meaning.

Talk about is a two-word verb.   **Talk about** means discuss.
Nathan: What did you and Susan talk about?
Karen: Their vacation in Hawaii.

Two-word verbs:

forget about   talk about
listen to   think about
look at   wait for
speak to   worry about
talk to   write to
look for

Time expressions with the ... before ...

It's Sunday night. **The night before last** was Friday night.
It's my third week at work. **The week before last** was my first week.
It's May. **The month before last** was March.
It's 2002. **The year before last** was 2000.

What did you do the night before last?

I wrote to my family.

I'm worried about my future.

Communication Goals	Grammar Goals	Vocabulary Goals
Explaining wishes and desires	Contrasting *would like to +* verb with *like to +* verb	Feelings
Talking about ability	*Know how to +* verb	*Let me think about it.*
Expressing dissatisfaction and concern		*Not really.*
		What else?

1 Warm Up

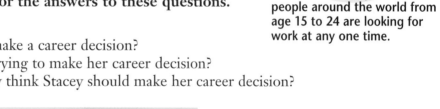

CULTURE UP CLOSE

A. **PAIR WORK** Discuss. What job do you do, or what would you like to do in the future? How did you make your decision?

B. Stacey and Casey are talking about making career decisions. Listen for the answers to these questions.

An estimated sixty million people around the world from age 15 to 24 are looking for work at any one time.

1. Who wants to make a career decision?
2. How is Stacey trying to make her career decision?
3. How does Casey think Stacey should make her career decision?

C. **PAIR WORK** Discuss with your partner. Which way to make a career decision is better?

2 Conversation

What should I do?

Phil Chen is talking to a career counselor.

A. Listen and practice.

1. Tell me about yourself, Phil.

Well, I'm studying graphic arts at UCLA. I'm graduating in June.

2. UCLA? I often counsel students from UCLA.

Yeah, my roommate ca[...] to see you a few years [...] His name's Mike Cohe[...]

Of course! I remember Mike. Well, it's a small world.

So, what else can you tell me about yourself?

I like to work with people, and I know how to speak Chinese.

3. That's excellent. It's good to speak another language. So, how can I help you? Why do you think you need career counseling?

4. Well, I'm worried about my future. So many jobs are disappear[...] and I want a job that will still be [...] here in the future.

You're an artist. You must be creative. Would you like to work in advertising?

Well, I'd like t[...] earn a good sala[...] and get benefit[...]

Graphic designers in advertising make good money. Just take a look at some of the job opportunities for that field on the Internet.

5. Okay. Let me t[...] about it. Tha[...]

Good luck. Oh—and say hi to Mike.

B. PAIR WORK Discuss.

1. Why is Phil seeing a counselor?
2. What qualifications do you think are necessary in advertising?

3 Grammar in Context

Explaining wishes and desires

Contrasting *would like to* + verb with *like to* + verb

Use *would like to* + verb to *express* wishes or desires in the future.

Use *like to* + verb to *explain* general desires or preferences.

Counselor:	What **would** you **like to** do, Phil?
Phil:	I don't know, but I **like to** work with people, and I **like to** draw.
Ben:	Where **would** Karen and Nathan **like to** go on their next vacation?
Annie:	I think they**'d like to** go to Paris.
Ben:	Why **would** they **like to** go to Paris?
Annie:	Because he **likes to** go to museums, and she **likes to** go shopping.
	They **don't like to** lie on the beach all day—they're city people.

Practice

A. PAIR WORK Take turns. Ask and answer questions about why the following people wish to do these things.

Example: *Brad / work for an international company // travel to new places*

1. Brad / buy a car // drive
2. Jason / be an actor // act
3. Casey / be a doctor // help people
4. Nathan and Karen / stay home next vacation // travel a lot
5. Ben / buy a guitar // play music

Why would Brad like to work in an international company?

Because he likes to travel to new places.

B. PAIR WORK Take turns. Write two questions about the future. Ask your partner the questions, then write his or her answers.

 Interact

C. PAIR WORK Find out about a classmate's preferences. Look at the list of activities, and write your own preferences and your partner's preferences for each one.

Activities	My partner's preferences	My preferences
1. eat for dinner tonight		
2. read		
3. watch on TV		
4. do this weekend		
5. do on vacation		
6. do during lunch hour tomorrow		
7. do in a big city		
8. do in the country		
9. listen to on the radio		
10. buy when you go shopping next time		

D. Report some of your preferences to the class.

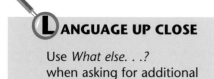

LANGUAGE UP CLOSE

Use *What else. . .?* when asking for additional information.

4 Grammar in Context

Talking about ability

To talk about ability, use *know how to* + verb

Counselor: Would you like to work in advertising?

Phil: Not really. I don't **know how to** sell.

Counselor: The advertiser doesn't sell. He makes the product attractive.

Phil: I **know how to** do that. I can make anything look good. What else should I **know how to** do?

Counselor: Well, you must **know how to** work well with people, too.

Practice

A. Match the abilities to the appropriate occupations.

1. draw well   ____ translator

2. plan buildings   ____ chef

3. make good food   ____ architect

4. design web pages   ____ webmaster

5. speak foreign languages well   ____ graphic designer or artist

B. Write four sentences about the different occupations above.

Example: *A chef must **know how to** make good food.*

 ## Interact

C. PAIR WORK Take turns asking and answering questions about job preferences and abilities for different professions.

> Would you like to be an architect?

> Not really. I don't know how to plan buildings.

D. GROUP WORK Talk about your job preferences and abilities with your classmates. Tell each other about things you would and wouldn't like to do.

5 Vocabulary in Context

Expressing dissatisfaction and concern

Annie: What's the matter, Ben?

Ben: I guess I'm **bored with** my work.

Annie: Why don't you get a part-time job?

Nathan: Is there something wrong, Karen?

Karen: I don't know. I guess I'm **upset with** my boss.

Casey: What's the matter, Jason?

Jason: I guess I'm **tired of** acting. All the jobs I get are the same.

Brad: What's wrong, Mike?

Mike: I'm **worried about** Ken. He can't find a full-time position.

Brad: Why doesn't he look on the Internet?

Practice

A. Use the expressions from the box to complete the following conversations. Your answers will vary.

A: You don't look very happy. _____?

B: I don't know. _____ studying.

A: Why don't you _____?

B: You don't look very happy. _____?

A: I guess _____?

B: Why don't you _____?

B. PAIR WORK Practice the conversations.

CULTURE UP CLOSE

The happiest workers in the world live in Denmark. Sixty-two percent of Danes say they are happy at work.

Pronunciation

C. Listen and repeat these questions and answers.

1. What's the matter?
   I don't know. I guess I'm bored with my job.
2. What's the matter?
   I don't know. I guess I'm tired of this city.

D. Now practice these sentences with the same intonation.

1. I guess I'm bored with this town.
2. I guess I'm tired of this weather.
3. I guess I'm upset with my sister.
4. I guess I'm tired of this food.
5. I guess I'm bored with this place.
6. I guess I'm worried about my future.

Interact

E. GROUP WORK Talk to a few classmates. Take turns finding out about each other's dissatisfaction with something. Use real or imaginary things. Then tell the class what you learned about your classmates.

6 Listening in Context

Stacey is making an appointment to visit a career counselor.

A. Listen for the following specific information.

1. What is the name of the counselor she will see?
2. What day will she go?
3. What time is her appointment?

B. Listen again. Why is Stacey making the appointment? What's the matter?

C. PAIR WORK Discuss with your partner. What questions do you think the counselor will ask Stacey? What do you think her answers will be?

D. GROUP WORK What advice would you give Stacey about changing her job? What kind of job would you recommend for Stacey? Discuss your reasons with your classmates.

7 Reading

Job search

Before you read

A. Phil Chen is looking for a job on the Internet. What job categories should he choose? What keywords should he use to search for a job? Why?

B. PAIR WORK What job categories would you and your partner choose? What keywords would you use? Why?

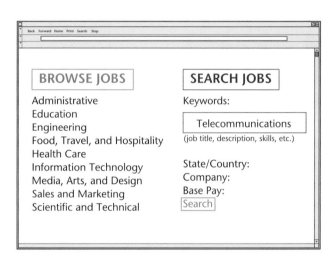

BROWSE JOBS	SEARCH JOBS
Administrative	Keywords:
Education	
Engineering	Telecommunications
Food, Travel, and Hospitality	(job title, description, skills, etc.)
Health Care	
Information Technology	State/Country:
Media, Arts, and Design	Company:
Sales and Marketing	Base Pay:
Scientific and Technical	Search

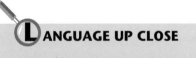

LANGUAGE UP CLOSE

On the Internet, use *Browse* to see general information.
Use *Search* to find specific information.

While you read

C. What kind of information appears in these job ads?

useful abbreviations
yrs = years
w/ = with
exp. = experience

Graphic Designer	Advertising Industry	We seek an individual who will be responsible for creative graphic productions. Must have college degree, w/ 2 yrs. exp. using graphic and DTP software. Competitive salary, full-time.	The Look, New York, NY HR@The Look
Graphic Design	Consulting Industry	College student or grad, internship, graphic software experience, to create business logos.	Rougeman & Associates, San Francisco, CA HR@rouge
Graphics Designer	Telecom-munications	College degree, 1-3 yrs. exp. in computer design. Full-time position. Will create label designs, logos, and trademark symbols.	Comreach Mobile, San Diego, CA Jobs@comobile
Graphics Designer	Advertising	1 yr. exp., excellent communication skills, college degree, proficient with graphics software; will be planning and producing creative graphics and visual images, $33,000-$36,000.	Marketing Inc. Los Angeles, CA Guru@market

After you read

D. Answer the questions.

1. What types of companies are hiring graphic designers?
2. Where are the companies located?
3. Do they all give the same information? What are some of the differences?
4. What requirements appear in all the ads?

8 Writing

Job query

Before you write

A. PAIR WORK **Choose one of the job ads on page 94. Reread it carefully. Discuss the answers to these questions.**

1. What information does the ad give?
2. What other information would you like to have about this job?

Write

B. Write an e-mail asking for this information.

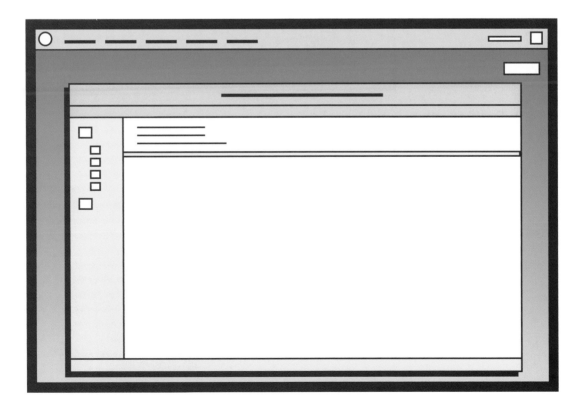

A. PAIR WORK Student A: Look at the chart and the ads for two job openings below. Student B: Look at the chart and the ads for two job openings on page 127. Take turns asking and answering the appropriate questions to fill out your chart with the information from your partner's ads.

	Job opening 1	Job opening 2
Job title		
Academic requirments		
Experience		
How to apply		

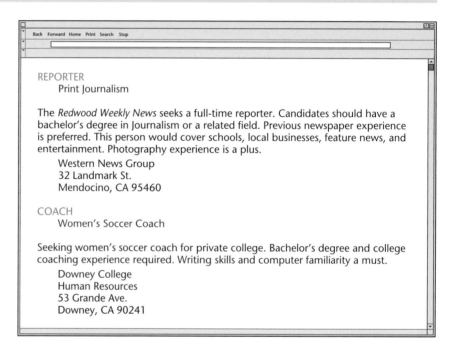

REPORTER
Print Journalism

The *Redwood Weekly News* seeks a full-time reporter. Candidates should have a bachelor's degree in Journalism or a related field. Previous newspaper experience is preferred. This person would cover schools, local businesses, feature news, and entertainment. Photography experience is a plus.

Western News Group
32 Landmark St.
Mendocino, CA 95460

COACH
Women's Soccer Coach

Seeking women's soccer coach for private college. Bachelor's degree and college coaching experience required. Writing skills and computer familiarity a must.

Downey College
Human Resources
53 Grande Ave.
Downey, CA 90241

B. GROUP WORK Report back to the group.

Stay **TUNED**

Suite 900-940 →
← Suite 960-980

Where's Phil going?

What did she say?

Communication Goals	Grammar Goals	Vocabulary Goals
Reporting what someone said Talking about periods of time Describing personal qualities	Reported speech Prepositions: *from, until, during*	Personal qualities *What about you?* *He's interviewing for a job.* *It was nice meeting you.*

1 Warm Up

A. What information appears on Phil Chen's resume? What else would you like to know about Phil if you were inteviewing him? Make a list.

Resume

Phillip Chen
Hollywood Oaks Apts.
607 Mansfield Rd., Apt. 4
Los Angeles, CA 90120
Telephone: (310) 555-7869

Education
1998-2001	Major: Graphic Arts; Degree: B.A. University of California at Los Angeles
1994-1997	Oakland High School, Oakland, CA

Special Honors   Class president; Honor Society

Experience
June–September 2000	Tour Guide, Film Industry Museum, Hollywood, CA
October 1997–May 1998	Waiter at Salads of the Stars, Hollywood, CA

Travel
May–September 1997	Taiwan

Languages   Excellent Chinese oral skills, fair written skills

References   Eugene Park, Professor of Fine Arts, UCLA
Mike Cohen, Webmaster, Smith and James, Inc.

B. Look at your list from *A*. Think of three interview questions to ask Phil.

C. Discuss. How does your educational and work experience compare to Phil's?

2 Conversation

Did you get the job?

Phil Chen is interviewing for a job as a graphic designer.

A. Listen and practice.

1. So, Phil, you said you were a student.

That's right. I'm studying graphic arts at UCLA.

And I see you worked at a museum last summer.

2. Yes. I worked as a part-time guide from Jun until September. I did some drawings there.

3. Would you like to see them? I have them right here.

4. Why, Phil, these are wonderful. Your art teacher said you were a good student. But you're also a very talented artist.

Thank you.

5. Unfortunately, we don't have any job openings now.

job openings = available positions

6. If I have a job opening soon, I'll contact you. I like your work a lot.

That's great. Thank you very much. It was nice meeting you.

And it was very nice meeting you, too.

So, Phil, how was the interview? Did you get a job?

Well, she said she liked my work, but I don't know. She also said they didn't have any openings right now.

B. Who is recommending Phil for a job? How do you know this? Circle the words in the conversation that tell you.

3 Grammar in Context

Reporting what someone said

Direct speech vs. reported speech

Brad:	What did the director say about your audition?	Brad:	What else did she say?
Jason:	She **said** I **was** very talented.	Jason:	She **said** she **had** to see a lot of other actors.

Direct speech / Present tense	**Reported speech / Past tense**
Director: "You **are** very talented."	The director **said** Jason **was** talented.

Practice

A. PAIR WORK Take turns. Read each exchange. Report what each person said.

Example: Brad: "You look very worried."
Jason: "I'm just tired and hungry."
A: *Brad said Jason looked very worried.*
B: *Jason said he was just tired and hungry.*

1. Brad: "This sandwich is very good."
Jason: "Yes, mine is great, too."
2. Jason: "There are a lot of actors auditioning for this role."
Brad: "I'm sure there are."
3. Jason: "But I really want to get it."
Brad: "It's a great role."
4. Jason: "The producer is a very busy person."
Brad: "All producers are very busy."

Interact

B. GROUP WORK Take turns. Make a statement about yourself. Report one of your classmate's statements to another classmate.

Example: **A:** *"I'm very hungry."*
B: *What did Carlos say?*
C: *Carlos said he was very hungry.*

4 Grammar in Context

Talking about periods of time

Prepositions: *from, until, during*

Use **from . . . until . . .** to say when something begins and ends. Use **during** to talk about what was going on in a specific period of time.

Interviewer:	How long did you work as a model?
Stacey:	For almost two years. **From** August 1999 **until** May 2001.
Casey:	How are you feeling, Stacey?
Stacey:	I'm OK now, but I was very nervous **during** the interview.

Practice

A. PAIR WORK Use information from Phil's resume on page 97 to ask and answer questions about when and where he did certain things.

Example: **A:** *When did Phil go to high school?*
B: *From 1994 until 1997.*

B. Complete the following sentences with *in, on, at, during,* or *until.*
More than one answer may be correct.

1. Mike and Ken are going to play soccer _____ Saturday.

2. Phil had to wait _____ the end of the week for an interview.

3. Everybody laughed a lot _____ the movie.

4. _____ 4:00 all of Susan's students go home.

5. Brad is always bored _____ his math class.

6. Andy is on vacation. He doesn't go to bed _____ 10:00.

7. Casey is never nervous _____ a test.

8. Nathan and Karen are planning a trip _____ July.

Interact

C. PAIR WORK Write down five important events in your past; for example, *I went to high school, I learned to play the guitar, I lived in New York, I had a part-time job.* Work with a partner. Look at his or her list of events and ask at least two questions about each event.

How long did you live in Bangkok?

For three years.

When did you move there?

In 1998.

D. GROUP WORK Tell the class about one very interesting event on your partner's list.

5 Vocabulary in Context

Describing personal qualities

1. Karen likes to help people. She listens to their problems. She is very **caring**.

2. Jason and Casey like to meet and talk to new people. They are **outgoing**.

3. Nathan never spends too much money, and he doesn't like to do anything dangerous. He's always very **careful**.

4. Susan teaches many students. Sometimes her students don't understand and ask the same questions again and again. She is always polite to them. Susan is very **patient**.

5. Ben likes to write. His stories are exciting and interesting. He is very **creative**.

6. Annie exercises a lot. She is never tired. She's very **energetic**.

7. Brad studies very hard. He loves reading and thinking about new ideas. He's very **studious**.

8. Kevin always does what he says he's going to. People can always trust him. He's a **reliable** person.

Practice

A. What personal qualities do you think people in the following occupations should have? Write one or two adjectives that describe each job.

1. actor
2. model
3. athlete
4. doctor
5. nurse
6. teacher
7. engineer
8. student
9. artist
10. pilot

B. Write a sentence or two about each occupation.

Example: *Actors work with many people. They should be **outgoing** and **energetic**.*

C. GROUP WORK Read at least one of your sentences to the class. Does everyone agree?

In the United States, it's generally not allowable to ask people their age when they apply for a job.

 Interact

D. PAIR WORK Make a list of your personal qualities. Tell your partner how these qualities match your present or future occupation.

 **Listening in Context**

A. Jobseek is a national recruiting firm. They interview job applicants for many companies. They are currently seeking people to fill two of the job openings below. Listen to the telephone conversations and check the job openings you hear.

B. Listen again and fill in the requirements for each job mentioned.

Jobseek			
An equal opportunity recruiter			
Job openings	**Education**	**Experience**	**Personal qualities**
Receptionist			
Teaching assistant			
Webmaster			
Mechanic			

C. GROUP WORK Do you think the candidates mentioned will do a good job? Why?

LANGUAGE UP CLOSE

An *equal opportunity employer/recruiter* gives an equal chance to all qualified applicants, male or female, of any age, ethnicity, or social status.

Tomorrow's workers

Before you read

A. PAIR WORK Discuss with a partner. Has computer technology or the Internet changed your life? If so, how?

 ## While you read

B. Circle all the work-related words you find as you read the article.

The Workforce of Tomorrow

Thomas Baker, the head economist at Avery National Laboratories, said at the Global Meeting for Work Research, "The world of work is changing." He said that technology had not only changed the way we work today, but will change the way we work tomorrow.

"Our workplace is changing. Our jobs are changing. And our professions are changing," he said. He described tomorrow's workers in the following way:

They love their work!
Their work is important!
They are adventurers!
They want to make a difference!

> to make a
> difference =
> change or
> influence
> things to make
> them better

They put their resumes on the Web and keep them updated. They find all their jobs on the Web. They get their training on the Web. They create wonderful projects with teammates around the world on the Web. They manage their careers on the Web with fantastic personal websites.

They work at home. They work with companies and partners in 14 countries. They attend six to ten virtual meetings every week, and they're studying for advanced degrees at virtual universities. They are very happy with their jobs and with their lives.

After you read

C. GROUP WORK Discuss the following questions with your group.

1. Do you agree with the writer's description of tomorrow's workers? Why or why not?
2. Do you think all workers in the future will have the same qualities as "tomorrow's workers"? Why or why not?

Writing

An online resume

Before you write

A. PAIR WORK What does it mean to post your resume online? Discuss the advantages and disadvantages of doing this.

Write

B. Fill in the form below to complete your online resume.

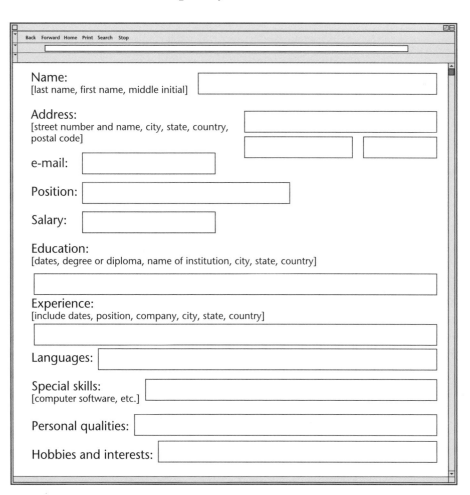

9 Putting It Together

A. Think of one type of work that you would like to do. Write the job title in the top left of the chart below.

B. What skills and qualifications are required for this job? Write the requirements in the numbered spaces in the left column of the chart.

C. GROUP WORK Work with your group to fill in each other's charts. Write your group members' names in the chart. Ask them if they would be able to meet these requirements. Write *yes* or *no* in each box next to the job requirement.

Job title	Name	Name	Name	Name
Job requirements	Yes or No	Yes or No	Yes or No	Yes or No
1.				
2.				
3.				
4.				

Stay **TUNED**

Why is Nathan getting into shape?

You're doing beautifully!

Communication Goals	Grammar Goals	Vocabulary Goals
Talking about sports / hobbies	Adverbs, regular and irregular	Sports
Describing actions	*as* + adverb + *as*	*He's in great shape.*
Comparing how people do things		*He'll do well.*
		She beat them all.

1 Warm Up

A. **Look at the pictures. Match the words below with each picture. Are you good at any of these sports?**

swimmer	basketball player	runner
soccer player	skier	tennis player

B. **Listen to Susan and Andy talking about a sports match. Circle the words you hear. What sport are they talking about?**

win	won	lose	lost	beat
opponents	player	team	tournament	bat

2 Conversation

Go, Nathan!

A. Look at the story and listen.

Nathan is running a 10K race. His friends are watching.

1.

Where's Nathan? I don't see him.

There he is. Nathan's doing very well.

But he's running slowly now. I think he's tired.

2.

Oh, no. He's in great shape. He'll do well. You'll see.

Yeah, he's a very good runner.

That's for sure.

3.

He's going as fast as he can.

Hurry, Nathan! Run!

Pass them! Pass them!

4.

175

101

You're doing beautifully. Go, Nathan! Go! Go!

5.

175

101

6.

He came in first!

He beat them all!

He won! Nathan won!

that's for sure= you're right

B. Discuss. What distance did Nathan run? How did Nathan's friends describe him?

3 Grammar in Context

Describing action

Adverbs

Adverbs describe how someone does something.

He plays **well.**
She dances **beautifully.**

Regular adverbs are formed by adding -ly to an adjective.
quick + -ly = *quickly*   *beautiful* + -ly = *beautifully*

Some examples of irregular adverbs are: *fast, hard,* and *well.*

A. Read the sentences.

Karen plays chess **well.**

Ben sings **badly.**

Stacey dances **beautifully.**

Casey swims **slowly.**

Mike walks **quickly.**

Ben writes **carefully.**

Practice

B. **Complete the sentences with an adverb.**

1. Hurry up! Run _____ or we will lose the race.
2. Annie cooks _____, so I hope she doesn't invite me to dinner at her place.
3. Please speak _____. I can't understand you.
4. Move that table _____, it's made of glass!
5. Tom plays cards _____. He always wins.
6. Sharon paints _____. She won a scholarship to art college.

Scholarship = money to pay for a student's education

Interact

C. PAIR WORK Make a list of things you do well, badly, carefully, slowly, quickly, or beautifully. Take turns talking about the things on your lists.

LANGUAGE UP CLOSE

What people in the U.S. call *soccer,* most people around the world call *football.* What Americans call *football* is known outside the U.S. as *American football.*

4 Grammar in Context

Comparing how people do things

As + adverb + *as*

Use **as** + adverb + **as** to compare how people do things.

1. Ted swims 100 meters in 1 minute.
   Larry swims 100 meters in 1 minute. } Larry swims **as fast as** Ted **does.**

2. Hajime swims very fast.
   Gino swims pretty fast. } Gino **doesn't** swim **as fast as** Hajime **does.**

3. I can skate very well.
   Bob can skate pretty well. } Bob **can't** skate **as well as** I **can.**

4. I speak Spanish well.
   You speak Spanish very well. } I **don't** speak Spanish **as well as** you **do.**

They play tennis **as well as**	I you we they	do.	He can speak Spanish **as well as**	I you he she	can.
They don't ski **as well as**	he she	does.	She can't play piano **as well as**	we they	

Practice

A. Todd and Taylor enjoy the same hobbies, but they each do some things better than the other. Look at the chart. Make sentences to compare how well Todd and Taylor do the things below.

Interact

B. PAIR WORK Tell your partner how well you do the activities in the chart. Compare how well you do things with your partner.

Hobbies	Todd	Taylor
run	fast	fast
speak French	badly	well
cook	well	very well
drive	fast	carefully
ski	slowly	beautifully
play guitar	well	badly

Pronunciation

C. **Listen to the stressed words.**

Example: *Be as good as you can today.*

D. **Listen. Circle the stressed word.**

1. Complete the forms as neatly as you can.
2. Try to work as quickly as possible.
3. Bring a doctor as fast as you can.

4. Leave as quickly as possible.
5. Be as patient as you can with your friends.
6. Drive as slowly as possible on icy roads.

E. **Listen again and repeat.**

F. **Write sentences using *as . . . as* to give advice for each of the following occupations. Use the sentences in D as models.**

swimmer	ballet dancer	soccer player	student	teacher	writer

1. _____
2. _____
3. _____

5 Vocabulary in Context

Sports scores

win / won the race

beat / beat the opposition

lose / lost the game

finish / finished in third place

tie / tied for first place

come in / came in second

Practice

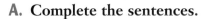

A. Complete the sentences.

Speech bubble: How did the Penguins do last night?

Speech bubble: They tied with the Pirates, 2 to 2.

1. My brother is an excellent batter. He _____ the game for his team.

2. The Mexican and the British runners had exactly the same time.

   They _____ for second place.

3. Korea _____ Spain in the soccer final.

4. If our team _____, we will be very sad.

5. Did she _____ first or second in the marathon?

6. Joanne _____ second in the championships.

B. PAIR WORK Look at the sports results listed at right. Work with a partner to ask and answer questions about the scores.

> **Today's Sports News**
>
> **Tennis**
> Costas vs. Armstrong (6 – 1, 4 – 6, 7 – 5, 5 – 7, 6 – 2)
>
> **Soccer**
> Riverview 2, Middletown 0
>
> **Baseball**
> Panthers 0, Devils 2
>
> **Ice hockey**
> Penguins 2, Pirates 2
>
> **Basketball**
> Pacific 105, Atlantic 100
>
> **Figure skating**
> Gold: Lim; Silver: Hughes; Bronze: Alexi

6 Listening in Context

A. Chris and Brenda are talking about their sports abilities. Circle the sports you hear.

baseball   badminton   ice skating
soccer   tennis   volleyball

B. Listen again. Circle the correct answer.

1. Brenda and Chris take tennis lessons twice a week.
   a. true   b. false

2. Chris is a better tennis player than Brenda.
   a. true   b. false

3. Brenda can't play volleyball well.
   a. true   b. false

4. Chris can play badminton well.
   a. true   b. false

C. PAIR WORK Talk to a partner about the activities and sports you like. How often do you do these activities? How good are you at each one?

A great soccer star

Before you read

A. GROUP WORK Discuss. What sports do people in your country enjoy most? Who are the most famous sports stars in your country?

While you read

B. Complete the chart with information about the soccer player.

outstanding =
very
good/special

training =
an exercise
program

Last name _____
First name _____
Place of birth _____
Year of birth _____
Training experience as a boy

_____

_____

Age at first match for the national team _____
Retirement age _____

score a goal

retire = stop
working /
stop playing a
sport

Edson Arantes was born in 1940 in Brazil. He was an outstanding soccer player, but as a boy he had no formal training in the sport. He learned to play soccer by kicking a ball around with his friends on the beaches of Río de Janeiro. His first match for the Brazilian national soccer team was in 1955, and by 1958 he was a world-famous soccer player. From 1956 to 1968 he scored 1,200 goals for the Santos Club in Brazil and the Brazilian national team. He played for Brazil in four World Cup matches, and Brazil won three of these.

Everybody loved to watch him play. He was an excellent athlete and a wonderful team member. He was funny, too. He retired from Brazilian soccer in 1974, and the next year he went to the United States to play for the New York Cosmos. He helped to make the Cosmos team a very good one. He retired from soccer in 1977. He is considered one of the greatest soccer players of all time. In case you haven't guessed, Edson Arantes is better known to the world by his nickname—Pelé.

After you read

C. GROUP WORK Discuss. Why did everyone love to watch Pelé play? Which sports player or famous athlete would you like to watch? Why?

 **Writing**

A sports star

Before you write

A. PAIR WORK Think of a famous sports star. Describe this person to your partner, but do not say who it is. See if your partner can guess.

 Write

B. Write a paragraph about the sports star.

9 Putting It Together

A. GROUP WORK Look at the adjectives and adverbs in the box. Match the opposites.

cold	carelessly
interesting	well
happily	calmly
quickly	boring
dirty	loudly
bad	big
small	good
nervously	clean
softly	hot
badly	sadly
carefully	slowly

CULTURE UP CLOSE

John Stephen Akhwari of Tanzania entered the stadium of the 1968 Mexico City Summer Olympics injured and more than an hour after the winner of the marathon. His was the greatest last-place finish ever.

B. PAIR WORK Make a sentence with each of the words in the box above. Take turns.

Example: **A:** *My neighbors' children shout loudly.*

Stay TUNED

What does Mike really do at work?

What do you do?

Communication Goals	Grammar Goals	Vocabulary Goals
Expressing wishes	*Wish* + pronoun + *could*	Descriptive adjectives
Making logical conclusions	*Must be* for inferences	Computers
Making an inference		*I'm really swamped.*
		What exactly do you do?

1 Warm Up

A. Listen. Write the wishes in the spaces.

1. _____

2. _____

3. _____

B. PAIR WORK Compare your answers. Ask your partner about the wishes.

Example: **A:** *What does he wish he could do?*
           B: *He wishes he could . . .*

C. PAIR WORK Now ask your partner what three things he or she wishes for.

2 Conversation

I'm a webmaster.

A. Listen and practice

Mike Cohen is making a web page for the Hollywood Oaks Apartments.

1.

> Hi, Mike. You must be busy.

> Oh, hi, Annie. Yes. I've been really swamped lately.

> So, you're a webmaster. What exactly do you do in your job?

2.

> I wish I could understand computers better. Thanks or helping me with my web page.

> You're welcome.

3.

> I put websites on the Internet for businesses.

> You must be a computer genius.

> Not really.

4.

> So, what do you want on your web page?

> Well, there's going to be a vacancy in the building soon. I need to find a new tenant.

> Okay. Why don't you show the apartments and the pool on the web page?

5.

> I wish I could keep everyone here. There's such a great atmosphere in this building.

> I think everyone agrees with you.

swamped = really busy

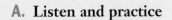

I just put your website onto the Internet a few minutes ago. Look! Two people are already asking for information about the apartment. They're singers from Brazil.

Singers? From Brazil? How interesting!

B. Answer the following questions.

1. How is Mike helping Annie?
2. What kind of tenants does she have at Hollywood Oaks?
3. What information does Annie want to put on the web page?

3 Grammar in Context

Expressing wishes

LANGUAGE **UP CLOSE**

Use *wish* to express something you would like to happen.

Wish + **pronoun** + *could* + **verb**

Could expresses ability or possibility.

I wish	I could	take a vacation.
He wishes	he could	run faster.

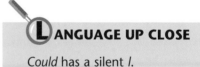

LANGUAGE **UP CLOSE**

Could has a silent *l*.

Practice

A. Use the following groups of words to express wishes.

1. he / swim better

   _____

2. they / take a vacation this summer

   _____

3. my sister / study dramatic arts

   _____

4. Annie / keep the same tenants at the Hollywood Oaks Apartments

   _____

B. Write a statement to express what each person wishes for.

1. Henri is a world class chef. He wants to win the 'Chef of the Universe' competition this year.

   _____

2. Susana is a real estate salesperson. She wants to start her own business.

   _____

3. Mihoko studies biochemistry. She wants to work as a lab technician.

   _____

4. Bertha has a new job in San Francisco, California. She is looking for a house there.

   _____

5. Juan likes to play chess. He wants to find someone to play with.

   _____

 ## Interact

C. PAIR WORK **Ask your classmates what they wish for in life. Use the topics below to help you.**

job	travel	sports	money
family	free time	home	romance

Example: **A:** *What jobs do you wish you could do?*
              B: *I wish I could work as a webmaster. How about you?*

4 Grammar in Context

LANGUAGE UP CLOSE

Use *must* + verb to say something that you believe to be true.

Making logical conclusions

Must + verb
You spend most of your free time working on the computer. You **must know** a lot about computers.
Enrique works as a volunteer in a hospital. He **must want** to be a doctor.

Practice

A. **Write sentences about what you believe to be true.**

1. Kenneth lives in Japan. (speak / Japanese)

   _____

2. Thomas works on a fishing boat. (be / good swimmer)

   _____

3. Angelica likes taking care of animals. (want to be / veterinarian)

   _____

4. My neighbor jogs every morning and goes to the gym in the afternoon.
   (like to / do exercise)

   _____

5. My sister works more than ten hours a day. (love / job)

   _____

Interact

B. **PAIR WORK** **Tell your
partner some information
about someone. Ask them to
say what they believe to be true
about the person.**

Pia knows a lot about computers.

She must use them a lot.

5 Vocabulary in Context

Making an inference

A. **Look at the list of adjectives to describe people. Find a word
in the box that means the opposite and write it in the blank.**

awful	big	bored	busy
early	happy	fast	short

1. excited _____
2. late _____
3. tall _____

4. sad _____
5. slow _____
6. small _____

Practice

B. PAIR WORK Take turns reading the first line of the conversations below. Respond to your partner using *must be* and one of the following words: *strong, tired, late, bored, busy, happy, sick, proud, excited, cold.*

So, I've got the job?

You must be very excited!

1. I slept only four hours last night.
2. My job is the same every day.
3. It's ten degrees outside. I forgot my jacket.
4. My brother won his last race.
5. My sister is getting married next week.
6. It's 9:05 and Frank isn't here. Where is he?
7. Sally carried these heavy boxes into the house.
8. I have a fever and a headache.
9. I spent all day cleaning the house.
10. Pam and Sue are running to class.

Interact

C. PAIR WORK Take turns making inferences about how each other feels using real events from your personal lives.

Example: **A:** *I have two important tests tomorrow.*
            B: *You must be nervous.*

6 Listening in Context

Talking about computers

A. Look at the computer as you listen to the conversation. Check off the parts as you hear their names.

CD-ROM Drive

mouse

internet

monitor

keyboard

B. Listen again. Answer the questions.

1. What will Joseph use the computer for?
2. Which of these items was mentioned but is not labeled in the photo?
   CD-writer   floppy disk drive   modem
3. How much does Joseph pay for his computer?

C. PAIR WORK Compare your answers with your partner.

D. PAIR WORK Role-play the conversation with a partner. Imagine you are buying a computer. What would you use it for? How much would you pay?

 CULTURE
UP CLOSE

The United States Department of Justice has a website at **cybercrime.gov** that tells you how to report information on computer criminals.

Reading

An encyclopedia entry

Before you read

A. PAIR WORK **Discuss the following questions with a partner:**

1. How would you rate your Internet knowledge?

excellent   good   fair   poor

2. What do you use the Internet for?

school work   to buy things   for fun

3. How many hours a week do you spend on the Internet?

none   1 – 5   6 – 10   11 – 15   16 - 20

4. What else would you like to know about the Internet?

_____

_____

 ## While you read

B. **Underline words or phrases that refer to what the webmaster does.**

After you read

C. **Write a definition for each word.**

  1. e-mail: _____

  _____

  _____

  2. webmaster: _____

  _____

  _____

  3. graphics: _____

  _____

  _____

  4. experts: _____

  _____

---

webmaster: (n) a word which refers to a person who is responsible for a website. It can include people who run or monitor the site, supervise its content, and ensure that it is functioning correctly.

The webmaster is involved in building or designing web pages and keeps the graphics, programming, and content up to date. Some webmasters have little knowledge about the content and only handle the technical problems that occur. They have support from other people who are experts on the content of the website. The webmaster must also monitor the number of people who visit the site.

Any information or questions about the website are directed to this person and he/she must respond to all inquiries. When you see an e-mail address like this one: *info@domain.com,* it is usually for questions or information to be directed to the webmaster.

This term is not gender specific and can refer to a man or a woman or a group of people who work on a website.

D. Make a list of a webmaster's responsibilities. Use the words or phrases you underlined in the passage on page 124 to help you.

1. _____
2. _____
3. _____
4. _____
5. _____
6. _____

8 Writing

Designing a web page

Before you write

A. You want to publish something about your school on the Internet. Answer the following questions.

1. What is the purpose of your web page?
2. Who is going to visit your web page?
3. What will they want to find there?
4. What will they want to do there?

B. PAIR WORK Compare your answers to the above questions with a partner.

Writing

C. Write the content for your own web page. Combine your ideas with your partner's ideas. Make a final list of the information you want on your web page.

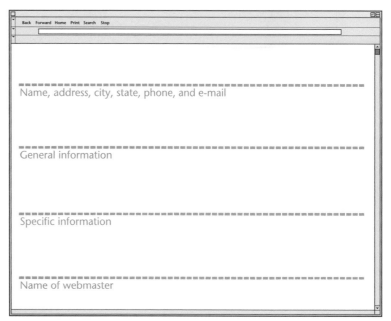

Name, address, city, state, phone, and e-mail

General information

Specific information

Name of webmaster

D. GROUP WORK Share your web page ideas with your classmates.

9 Putting It Together

A. Think of a well-known person, place, or thing.
Do not tell anyone what it is.

B. GROUP WORK Take turns. Give clues until your classmates
can guess the person, place, or thing. They can only use
the sentence "It must be ___" to make their guesses.
The person who guesses correctly takes the next turn,
letting the others guess.

Stay **TUNED**

Student B activities

Unit 6

Practice

C. PAIR WORK Student A, turn to page 61. Student B, look at the chart below. Complete the missing information in your chart by asking your partner questions.

Number of Miles Between Some U.S. Cities			
From	To Chicago	To Kansas City	To New York
Boston			206
Los Angeles		1,585	2,786
Seattle	2,013	1,839	
Washington, D.C.		1,043	

Unit 9

Putting it Together

A. PAIR WORK Student A, look at the chart and the ads for two job openings on page 96. Student B, look at the chart and the ads for two job openings below. Take turns asking and answering the appropriate questions to fill out your chart with the information from your partner's ads.

	Job Opening 1	Job Opening 2
Job Title		
Academic Requirements		
Experience		
How to Apply		

ELECTRICAL ENGINEER

Engineering

Electrical Engineer to develop and test electrical instruments and systems. Bachelor of Science in electrical engineering or equivalent is required.

Field Words
Paris, TX
HR@FieldWorks

CHEF

Restaurant industry

Willow Restaurant seeks a qualified sous chef. Candidate must have a minimum of 3-5 years cooking experience in a fine dining establishment. Management skills a plus. Salary depends on experience. Excellent benefits.

Rita Besco
33 Frost St.
Newport, RI 02840

Vocabulary - Unit 1

Nouns	Adjectives/Adverbs	Verbs	Expressions
action	funny	hand	Did you have a good time?
an audience	often	laugh	Get home.
a comedy	only	restrict	It was OK.
a date	wrong		It was scary.
a drama			I closed my eyes.
guidance			I'd love to.
a horror movie			I blew it!
a monster			I stayed home.
a rock concert			
a science fiction			
movie			
a territory			
a western			

Vocabulary - Unit 2

Nouns	Adjectives/Adverbs	Verbs	Expressions
a bus station	glad	prefer	I'm really sorry.
a cellular phone	main	turn	I'm so glad.
a coat	near	sightsee	How do I get to...?
a college	north		It's right there.
a commuter train	south		It's great to see you!
directions			
a fire department			
a map			
a museum			
a park			
a police station			
a post office			
a subway			
a subway line			
a supermarket			
a telephone			
company			
a train station			
a town			

Vocabulary - Unit 3

Nouns	Adjectives/Adverbs	Verbs	Expressions
caffeine	always	disagree	I am in great shape.
a chart	average	eat out	Really?
an excuse	easy	go away	Why don't we...?
an exercise	hardly ever	improve	Slow down.
fish	healthy	jog	Yeah, right.
fruit	low fat	lift	How often...?
a gym	never	lose	
a habit	obese	work out	
heart disease	overweight		
junk food	physical		
a percentage	regularly		
a push-up	seldom		
red meat	sometimes		
a researcher	thin		
a routine			
a sit-up			
a suggestion			
vegetables			
weights			

Vocabulary - Unit 4

Nouns	Adjectives/Adverbs	Verbs	Expressions
a belt	attractive	exchange	They're on sale.
boots	better	fit	That's crazy.
cashmere	brown	spend	What's the problem?
curry	cheap		What's wrong with it?
a department store	expensive		
a fashion show	free		
gloves	long		
leather	loose		
a pair	pretty		
a scarf	recent		
silk	round		
a size	short		
a sleeve	spicy		
socks	sporty		
twins	tight		
a V-neck shirt	unhealthy		

Vocabulary - Unit 5

Nouns		Adjectives/Adverbs	Verbs	Expressions
a bag	jewelry	common	break	It's made of silver.
a bracelet	lycra	delicious	wrap	Can I help you with…?
a cabinet	metal	frightened		It's out of my price range.
cement	a milk jug	local		You're the greatest!
a century	a necklace	terrible		
a chair	nylon	worst		
Christmas	an opera			
clay	plastic			
cotton	polyester			
denim	a pot			
designer	a present			
clothing	a sauce			
a dish	silver			
earrings	steel			
fireworks	a toy			
a game	a variety			
gold	a wallet			
Hanukkah	wool			

Vocabulary - Unit 6

Nouns		Adjectives/Adverbs	Verbs	Expressions
a bird	a meter	active	alter	It should rain tomorrow.
a chain	a mile	alone	climb	How far is it?
a corner	a part	ancient	collect	How long will it take?
a crater	a petroglyph	cultural	contact	How old is it?
an entrance	a plant	eastern	dominate	How high is it?
an eruption	a pound	endangered	feed	How deep is it?
a foot	a protection	geographical	fly	There are plenty of…
a flight	a pyramid	geological	follow	
height	a reservation	massive	permit	
a hike	sand	natural	stand	
hiking boots	sea level	open	view	
a honeymoon	sunscreen	positive		
an island	a superintendent	southward		
a kilometer	a temple			
a kilogram	a trail			
a landmark	an update			
a lava field	vegetation			
a lava flow	wildlife			
length				

Vocabulary - Unit 7

Nouns	Adjectives/Adverbs	Verbs	Expressions
an accomplishment	dangerous	cope	What about you?
a chore	least	dust	I think you should.
housework	stressful	iron	Have fun!
laundry		mow	Watch out!
a lawn		offer	Hurry up.
therapy		praise	
		rake	
		smooth	
		sweep	
		vacuum	
		water	

Vocabulary - Unit 8

Nouns	Adjectives/Adverbs	Verbs	Expressions
an agent	approximately	board	hit the beach
a dinosaur	out-of-the-way		
a gate	reluctant		
a guard			
a jungle			
luggage			
a miniskirt			
a package tour			
a passport			
roller skates			
a rollercoaster			
a seat			
a suitcase			
a ticket			
a ticket counter			

Vocabulary - Unit 9

Nouns	Adjectives/Adverbs	Verbs	Expressions
advertising	administrative	develop	Let me think about it.
benefits	competitive	disappear	Not really.
a candidate	full-time	private	What else?
a career	previous	seek	
a chef	proficient	test	
a coach	qualified		
a counselor	related		
dissatisfaction	required		
entertainment	scientific		
a [job] field	technical		
graphic arts	visual		
hospitality			
an individual			
an internship			
an instrument			
journalism			
a label			
a logo			
a product			
a production			
a qualification			
a reporter			
a salary			
a score			
software			
a symbol			
a system			
a translator			

Vocabulary - Unit 10

Nouns	Adjectives/Adverbs	Verbs	Expressions
an adventurer	advanced	manage	He's interviewing for a job.
an applicant	allowed	recommend	
a diploma	careful		
an economist	caring		
an honor	creative		
a laboratory	currently		
an opening	energetic		
a producer	fantastic		
a recruiter	outgoing		
a resume	part-time		
a reference	reliable		
	studious		
	talented		
	unfortunately		
	virtual		

Vocabulary - Unit 11

Nouns	Adjectives/Adverbs	Verbs	Expressions
badminton	badly	beat	He's in great shape.
a ballet dancer	beautifully	kick	He'll do well.
a bat	calmly	lose	
distance	carelessly	pass	
a [sports] final	clean	retire	
figure skating	dirty	win	
football	excellent		
ice hockey	fast		
an ice skater	loudly		
a marathon	noisily		
an opponent	once		
a player	outstanding		
a race	quickly		
a scholarship	slowly		
a tournament	twice		
	wonderful		

Vocabulary - Unit 12

Nouns	Adjectives /Adverbs	Verbs	Expressions
an atmosphere	fair	carry	I'm really swamped!
dramatic arts	poor	ensure	What exactly do you do?
gender	world-class	function	
a genius		monitor	
a keyboard		supervise	
a monitor			
a mouse			
a tenant			
a vacancy			
a volunteer			
a wish			

Up Close Characters

Name: Casey Walker   Age: 23
Occupation: Medical student at UCLA
Hobbies: Swimming, relaxing at the beach, going to the movies
Favorite food: Brownies

Name: Brad Garcia   Age 20
Occupation: Student of business at UCLA
Hobbies: Photography, exploring new places
Favorite food: Chocolate banana crepes

Name: Jason Garcia   Age: 23
Occupation: Actor, and works in restaurant
Hobbies: Basketball
Favorite food: Barbecued chicken

Name: Stacey Walker   **Age:** 23

Occupation: Model

Hobbies: Listening to music, jogging, and going dancing

Favorite food: Spinach salad

Name: Kevin Jordan   **Age:** 40

Occupation: Doctor – pediatrician

Hobbies: Watching videos

Favorite food: Steak and potatoes

Name: Andy Jordan   **Age:** 7

Occupation: Student at elementary school

Hobbies: Swimming and going to the beach

Favorite food: Pizza, chocolate sundaes

Name: Susan Miller-Jordan   **Age:** 36

Occupation: Homemaker and history teacher

Hobbies: Chess

Favorite food: Spaghetti

Name: Karen Sanders   Age: 33
Occupation: Nurse
Hobbies: Beach volleyball
Favorite food: Seafood

Name: Nathan Sanders   Age: 33
Occupation: Engineer
Hobbies: Running, cycling
Favorite food: Thai food

Name: Annie Davis   Age: 48
Occupation: Apartment manager
Hobbies: Karate, yoga, gardening
Favorite food: Sushi

Name: Ben Wilson   Age: 50
Occupation: Writer
Hobbies: Taking care of pet bird Sebastian,
cooking, jogging, surfing
Favorite food: Apple pie

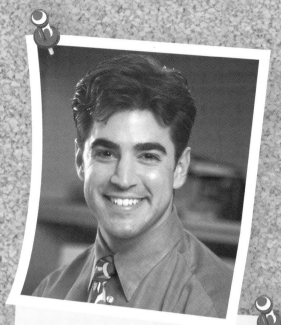

Name: Mike Cohen   **Age:** 27
Occupation: Web designer
Hobbies: Listening to music,
          computer games, hiking
Favorite food: Turkey and avocado sandwiches

Name: Ken Sato   **Age:** 23
Occupation: Exchange student
Hobbies: Skiing
Favorite food: Artichokes

Name: Phil Chen   **Age:** 22
Occupation: Student of graphic arts
          at UCLA
Hobbies: Painting
Favorite food: Waffles

What was a mime doing at the mall?

They say birds make the best pets in the world. Do you believe it?

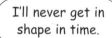

I'll never get in shape in time.